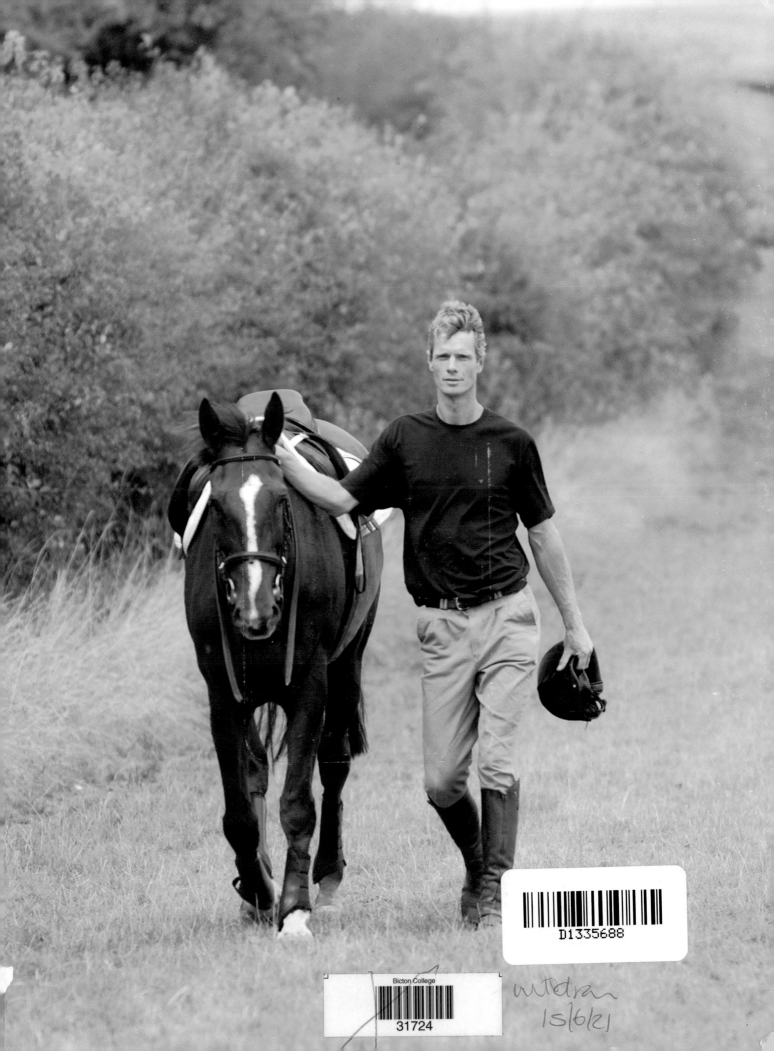

Schooling for Success

with William Fox-Pitt

Text • **Kate Green** Photography • **Kit Houghton**

D&C
David and Charles

A DAVID & CHARLES BOOK
Copyright © David & Charles Limited 2004, 2007

David & Charles is an F+W Publications Inc. company
4700 East Galbraith Road
Cincinnati, OH 45236

First published in the UK in 2004
First paperback edition 2007

Text copyright © William Fox-Pitt and Kate Green 2004, 2007

ISBN-13: 978-0-7153-1750-1 hardback
ISBN-10: 0-7153-1750-4 hardback

ISBN-13: 978-0-7153-2667-1 paperback
ISBN-10: 0-7153-2667-8 paperback

Printed in China by SNP Leefung
for David & Charles
Brunel House, Newton Abbot, Devon

Commissioning Editor   Jane Trollope
Art Editor   Sue Cleave
Project Editor   Jo Weeks
Desk Editor   Sarah Martin
Photography   Kit Houghton

Visit our website at www.davidandcharles.co.uk
David & Charles books are available from all good bookshops;
alternatively you can contact our Orderline on 0870 9908222 or
write to us at FREEPOST EX2 110, D&C Direct, Newton Abbot,
TQ12 4ZZ (no stamp required UK only); US customers call
800-289-0963 and Canadian customers call 800-840-5220.

Contents

Foreword by Yogi Breisner 7

Success Story 8

Flatwork 28

Jumping 50

Cross Country 66

At the Competition 138

Get Your Horse Fit 150

Index 160

Foreword

There are many good riders, some of whom become consistent winners but only a few of whom become consistent winners with style – William Fox-Pitt is one of these. This didn't come naturally to William, even though he has always had talent. I remember him as a teenager and, while he was very effective as a rider, one could not describe him as stylish.

Through hard work and dedication, William has developed into a competitive rider with an outstanding style, balance and effectiveness. The first steps for any young aspiring event rider to achieve the same are to understand the background, the ins and outs and the theories behind riding in general and cross-country in particular.

This book illustrates William's depth of knowledge when it comes to educating horses and improving one's riding. The tips will be valuable for any riders, from novice right up to international level, as the principles are the same for all.

YOGI BREISNER
British team manager

Yogi Breisner with the gold medal winning team at the Pau Europeans in 2001: William Fox-Pitt, Pippa Funnell, Jeanette Brakewell and Leslie Law.

Success Story

Eventing is perhaps the most popular of disciplines because its riding challenges are extremely varied and it's one of the few sports in which men and women can compete on equal terms, as can 'professionals' and 'amateurs'. You don't have to do it full time – the number of riders who have made it their career is relatively small compared to the overall number of participants – nor do you have to have a particular type of horse – one look at a horse inspection at a three-day event reveals the wide variety that are used for eventing. The sport caters for every aspiration, too, whether you want to complete a round at pre-novice level or to win Badminton; and to be successful every participant has to put in the same hours and endeavour – no matter who they are or what their level. You don't have to be winning – though winning Badminton must be the ultimate high – you can get a buzz simply from riding a five-year-old at his first event and reaching the finish.

A very good day – Ballincoola and Wallow, who were first and second at Bramham.

The special appeal of eventing is the thrill of riding across country; ask any rider and they will say there's no high like the one you feel at the end of a successful round. If we didn't love that, we'd all be doing either pure dressage or showjumping. However, the ultimate challenge is for you and your horse to go well in all three disciplines, and often this just doesn't happen. But at least you have three chances to have a good day (or days) – the first two phases might be awful, but if you go clear across country, you'll go home on a high, which

is far more satisfying than having to pack up after a disastrous five minutes in a dressage arena.

Just getting a horse to an event, sound and fit, requires a lot of work and so to complete should be considered an achievement in itself. But perhaps the real challenge of eventing is the opportunity to develop the

Owner Judy Skinner celebrates her horses Ballincoola and Wallow achieving a one-two at Bramham in 2003. Pictured are William, Judy's daughter, Lucy Payne, and Paul Trivett from Guardian Collections, sponsors of Bramham Horse Trials.

all-round expertise in both you and your horse. Because of increased safety measures anyone who becomes involved in the sport must be proficient in all three phases; no-one can progress without the necessary level of competence – and the work involved in achieving that competence must not be underestimated. You can no longer do as I did in the early days – simply get on a reasonably promising horse and stand a good chance of doing well. However, working to achieve all the different abilities required is fascinating because the focus is constantly changing; if one element goes well, there's always something else that needs to be done better. And all the while you are working not only to be able to perform all three disciplines to as high a standard as possible, but often to perform them all on the same day. Despite the keeness of the competition, the cameraderie in eventing is unique; riders are endlessly willing to help, generous with their advice and happy to give tips and walk courses with you.

My early years

I suppose it was inevitable that I would develop a love of horses. Both my parents competed at Badminton and my mother, Marietta, represented Britain in the 1967 European Championships; she was also second

Tamarillo, one of the most athletic horses William has ridden, at the 2002 World Games.

William, aged nine, aboard Knowlton Corona, his father's former Badminton horse, at the East Kent Pony Club one-day event.

at Burghley and fourth at Badminton – all before she took a break to have me at 28 years old. For my father, Oliver, horses were initially less prominent in his life due to his work commitments, but when he married my mother I think he realized it was better to join in than be left out. He thoroughly enjoyed his eventing and took it quite seriously for a time, completing Badminton and Burghley several times on a fairly difficult horse. As a child, I remember my parents competing, but they never got back to top level.

I am one of four children and we were all encouraged to ride from early on. My brother Andrew plays polo for the army and my sisters Laurella and Alicia evented. Andrew and I were involved in the Pony Club and we went hunting, which we very much enjoyed, but we certainly weren't pony mad; we liked getting on

and getting going, but the finer points of stable management and flatwork didn't figure very strongly. Despite our parents' depth of knowledge, they were careful not to kill our enthusiasm with the boring stuff and never bombarded us with technicalities.

At one time, Andrew and I had a pair of scruffy white ponies that lived out; we longed for brown ones that would look smart without all the washing. I can still remember the excitement of being allowed to have my horse clipped at the age of 14. We organized pony races – bareback and with only headcollars – and, inspired by a holiday in Wyoming, we decided that our Welsh Mountain ponies were going to become rodeo performers. We discovered that if we put a neckstrap around their loins and pulled it tight, they would buck. But after a while they were bucked out and, as hard as we pulled, they refused to leave the ground.

We were lucky in that although they weren't pretty or well-schooled, our ponies would jump. I now appreciate the amount of time and effort my mother must have put into driving around the country to find such suitable mounts. Being on something that actually wants to jump is the most important thing when learning the basics because it instils confidence. I wasn't very brave anyway – I usually had the quieter ponies, while Andrew had the mad ones.

Another advantage of my upbringing was that I rode lots of different horses. We had all sorts of ponies and green home-bred horses and were just expected to get on with it. As they weren't other people's horses, there was no pressure. When something went well, it was a personal achievement that boosted my confidence and when it didn't go well, it didn't really matter, it just meant that I would have to work harder.

I didn't have much style in those days – being tall and lanky – but I think I've always had a feeling for what a horse is doing – something that is hard to teach. You can learn to do most things in riding, but the knack of developing a feeling (for example, of exactly when to use your legs – and when not to) can, I believe, only come through experience.

It was a long time before anyone even worried about working on my style. I was completely unselfconscious and unaware of what I should and shouldn't be doing. Riding a horse on the bit or seeing a stride to a fence certainly wasn't what riding was about for me; in fact, I find it hard to remember when these details started to click. I do know that I learned about cross-country riding through hunting; my grandmother had a house in Leicestershire and I absolutely lived for hunting when I visited her. One Christmas holiday I had 15 days hunting and each evening would count up the fences I'd jumped, probably vastly exaggerating the total. My more technical knowledge of cross-country riding comes almost entirely from my mother.

The first time I rode at Badminton was in 1989, when there were no curving lines or complicated related distances on the cross-country course. Nowadays, such things are common. Five years previously, at the age of 15, I walked the show-jumping course at my first junior championships at Windsor with absolutely no consciousness of striding – my only worry was remembering the route. I'm sure that if I was doing the same with a child now, I'd be tempted to be saying, 'Count five strides in here and two there.' I saw dressage simply as a means of getting to the cross-country phase and my biggest concern was

Moon Man in typical relaxed mood, on the way to dressage at Kentucky in 2003.

The British Junior squad in 1985 – back row: Graham Law, Roland Lloyd-Thomas, Georgina Anstee, Sally Bateson, Jamie Railton, Alexandra Ramus; front row: William, Andrea Morris, Simon Hazlem, Melanie Hawtree, Clea Hoeg and Steven Chambers.

having to do six-and-a-half minutes of sitting trot. At the time I rode at Windsor, I'd only taken part in two novice competitions and one intermediate section – and I got long-listed! That would be unthinkable today, with all the politics, qualifications and safety rules attendant in the sport.

My tack consisted of a Stübben jumping saddle, a snaffle bridle and a cavesson noseband – for all three phases. Although this was 1984, when eventing had actually become quite 'modern', I would never have dreamed of asking for another bit and I'd never ridden in any type of saddle except a jumping one – it certainly didn't enter my head to ask about studs or boots. The late Colonel Lithgow, Chairman of the Junior Selectors

at the time, suggested to my mother that my horse should have a martingale because its head was so high it hardly saw its fences, to which she replied, 'Over my dead body!'

I feel lucky not to have had my early experiences of international competition complicated by technicalities, which exist now because of the way the sport has progressed and because of the increase in the standard of riding. Eventing for me was very simple – and fun. I still have the video of myself at Windsor – a lanky apparition fearlessly throwing the brave horse at the fences.

We have to accept that the sport has changed, but it's worth remembering the advantages that my generation – and earlier ones – enjoyed; we learned from our mistakes and we were given time by our supporters to put them right. We had fun, rather than being over-taught and encouraged to become adolescent perfectionists.

Above and below left: William and Steadfast were members of the British Junior team at the European Championships in Rome in 1987 where they won an individual silver medal.

Today, the sport is much more expensive, especially the training, and people tend to hunt less often because the horses are more valuable, which is a shame. There's far more competition, far more competitors and everything seems more urgent and serious – results count.

Steadfast, who began it all for me when I was 15, was bought by my mother. He came from Judy Bradwell, who thought he was a genuine sort and would be a useful horse for a boy to do novice events on. I wasn't at all enthusiastic about him as I thought he resembled a carthorse. I fancied the idea of the equivalent of a Mercedes to ride; Steadfast was probably a quarter Shire and he looked it. It seemed to me that there was nothing smart about him, including his name, and I was delighted when he failed the vetting

University days – the London Y team winning the BHS Challenge Trophy for University Riding Clubs in 1990. To William's left is Hannah Moody, now a dressage rider.

but, luckily as it turned out, my mother bought him anyway. It was one of the best decisions she made for me because, ultimately, Steadfast was responsible for me making a career with horses. My mother always had a good eye for a pony and in Steadfast she definitely saw something that no-one else had.

I got a dressage saddle, started learning to do sitting trot, and Steadfast took me to the Junior European Championships at Rotherfield in 1985 and then at Pratoni del Vivaro in Italy in 1987, where I won the individual silver medal. This was my first taste of a proper prize and it was a turning point because previously the only things I'd won tended to be 'best boy' awards at the Pony Club and fifth place rosettes. I was thrilled to do so well and, as I was on the point of leaving school, I suddenly felt that I could get into eventing properly.

Steadfast was an obvious team horse for the next stage, Young Riders (under-21s), and we were on the British team for three years in succession, winning two team gold medals and team silver. In the individual event we also won a bronze and came fourth twice, which was annoying because Steadfast was an incredibly consistent horse and if I'd known how to do

dressage, he'd probably have won three gold medals. Unfortunately, though, I was clueless. Having spent years unconcerned by the finer points of dressage, I now spent most of my time trying to keep Steadfast's head in the right place, something I now know isn't that difficult. Our team trainer Gill Watson had an uphill struggle with me because at the age of 17 I was trying to do something in which I had absolutely no heritage. Dressage was my weak link.

My student years

Unlike many of my team mates, I carried on riding while doing a degree in French at London University and I think this is why the break really happened for me. I was sent a couple of horses belonging to people who had given up, so I wasn't just riding my mother's horses. I had always been aware that I couldn't stay with my parents for ever, and this was the start of standing on my own feet.

I didn't have any income to finance my riding, but I was paid by these horses' owners to ride them, and at the time that seemed both a luxury and a very exciting development. It was great to be offered the ride on Faerie Sovereign, who turned out to be a useful back-up to Steadfast in my last year of Young Riders and which gave me a fantastic first ride at Burghley, and then Susanna Macaire offered me Briarlands Pippin. By 1990 I suddenly had three advanced horses, two of which weren't mine, which was even better. I acquired a small sponsorship deal, worth £5,000, from Smirnoff and I really thought I'd made it.

I still had the luxury of my horses being kept at home and prepared by my mother. This was crucial. Although it meant that I had life much easier than many of my contemporaries and avoided learning too many things the hard way, it gave me the security and time to be able to make up my mind about my career. I'm not a great worrier; at the time I believed it would all work out. I'm not sure my parents were so relaxed; I think they looked on my eventing as a game I would grow out of. However, I'd had a great education and had been made very aware that horses were not going to be a terrific source of income, so I really needed to work out whether I wanted to play at riding or throw myself into it. Having done Juniors and Young Riders, it made me hungry to give it a real go once I left university.

I was envious of the likes of my team mates Pippa Nolan (now Funnell), Kristina Gifford (now Cook) and Susanna Macaire, who had left school and were competing full time, and I realized I could never match them by riding only once every two weeks. But in the long-term it was an advantage to approach the sport from a more neutral standpoint and to know it was something I really wanted to do as well as afford to do.

At the beginning of 1992 I was approached by the clothing company Hackett who offered me sponsorship. This was on the strength of a good 1991 when I was made first reserve for the senior team for the Punchestown Europeans. (As part of my studies for my French degree, I had taken the horses over to Saumur in France in 1991 – it was the first time I'd had intensive training and it paid off.) I was 23 and I felt that if I was capable of attracting a sponsor, perhaps I could make a go of it and not live out of my parents' pockets – there was a strong feel-good factor about that. This was also the year of the Barcelona Olympics and, after my dressage training in France, I was feeling fired-up to have a good season.

I had two Badminton rides, Faerie Sovereign and Briarlands Pippin, and both won the big pre-Badminton advanced classes at Brigstock. But I was soon to discover the flip side of the sport because Faerie Sovereign went lame on the steeplechase at Badminton and Briarlands Pippin had to be put down after breaking his neck in a dreadful fall into the lake.

Sadly, it was back to the drawing board with

Steadfast, also off the road with a minor injury. However, later that year Sir Michael Turner offered me Chaka while his current rider Greg Watson was busy competing for Australia at the Olympics.

In 1993, my final year at university, I was given the ride on Chaka permanently and we had a great Badminton, finishing seventh. As a result, we were selected for the British team at the 1993 European Championships in Achselschwang, Germany. Barring Ginny Elliot, the senior squad were all first-time team members. Tina Gifford won a silver medal, but otherwise the competition was a total disaster for Britain. Nick Burton had a fall from Bertie Blunt and retired. And then Chaka was ill and had to be pulled up, so we

Chatsworth winner Stunning, with William's long-time head girl Jackie Potts

Chaka winning the Scottish Open at Thirlestane Castle, in 1994, the year in which he went on to win Burghley.

William with Stunning's owner Jayne Apter receiving the Doubleprint British Open trophy from the Princess Royal at Gatcombe in 2003.

made somewhat unfortunate history as the first British team not to complete a championship for years. Since the huge disappointment of my team debut, I have been lucky enough to win four team gold medals and a team bronze on four different horses.

My horses

Part of the unpredictability – and fascination – of eventing is that the typical event horse doesn't exist. Although conformation defects and temperament problems can preclude a horse being successful, event horses really do come in all shapes and sizes; the budding stars can end up being a disappointment, while the backward pupil can be transformed into the perfect end product. When you buy a horse for this sport you simply have to note all the good points and the bad ones and decide whether the pluses outweigh the minuses, because every horse has a downside. Two vital factors are that he has the temperament to want to do the work, and a conformation that will let him do it – after that, it's largely luck. The horses I've learned most from are the difficult ones – such as Steadfast, Chaka and Stunning, each of whom have contributed enormously to my riding today.

Steadfast was all heart but had less talent; he didn't have much scope and was further handicapped by a rider who had no eye for a stride. But I was his pupil and he felt he had a responsibility towards me; he was a one-off. Because of the way the sport has moved on, no-one who was really ambitious would buy him today and he probably wouldn't make it to Badminton. The days of schoolmaster horses like that being able to carry the younger riders are mostly gone.

In contrast, Chaka was all talent and came to me as a made horse, having been successfully brought out by Judy Herbert. Chaka was one of the scopey, all-round horses – good-looking with three great paces and capable of jumping a house. He wasn't scared of any fence – ditches or into-spaces – and he was more than capable of a clear show-jumping round. I'd never ridden

William and Stunning during their lap of honour after winning the World Cup qualifier at Chatsworth in 2003.

The British team at the Atlanta Olympics: William, Ian Stark, Karen Dixon and Gary Parsonage.

anything like it – his ability was way beyond my experience – sitting on him was like driving a Ferrari. But, on the downside, it was hard to convince him to go the extra mile for you.

I've never ridden such an enigmatic horse and after the consistency of Steadfast, I found Chaka extremely variable, especially mentally. I'd experienced disappointment and near-misses before but it was really something different to be seventh at Badminton in 1993 and then have the same horse put in two stops the following year, for no apparent reason. This experience made me realize that Chaka was more complicated than I thought and I decided that I needed to adopt a different approach. I'd always viewed him

with rose-tinted spectacles, thinking he was the best horse on earth, but our second Badminton really opened my eyes.

On returning home, I changed Chaka's fitness preparation, mixing interval and hill work, and I stopped thinking he was so marvellous. I rode him hard at Gatcombe and Thirlestane, and was second at both. Previously, I had run him sparingly, but now I realized that he was lazy and he needed outings to keep him on form. He had been my hope for the World Championships in The Hague, but the Badminton result had wiped out any chance of selection and so we went to Burghley instead, in a much sharper frame of mind. Winning Burghley was very exciting. Even though we were in the lead after the dressage, we were definitely not the favourites, and the commentators completely discounted him on cross-country day.

William and Moon Man, third and part of the successful British raid on the Rolex Kentucky four-star event in April 2003.

William and Tamarillo, members of the bronze medal winning team at the World Equestrian Games Jerez in 2002.

Owner The Hon Mary Guinness with her beloved Tamarillo at the 2002 World Equestrian Games in Jerez.

At Badminton in 1995 we so nearly did it again – we were in the lead after cross-country. However, Chaka was suddenly lame at the final trot-up. This was particularly sad because he really had given his best.

Stunning, owned by George and Jayne Apter, was the biggest challenge of all. When I started riding him, he was 13, the same age as Chaka, so he had quite a bit of history and also something of a reputation. He'd come from one of the best riders in the world – Mark Todd – who hadn't been able to get him around a four-star course, and I subsequently failed to get him around Badminton or Burghley.

Apart from the fact that he was racing-bred and incredibly fast, none of the phases came naturally to Stunning. He wasn't unhelpful or negative, but he was very unconfident. Surprisingly, having failed to complete Badminton and Burghley, he didn't completely lose confidence. When I abandoned the four-star plan and went back to three-star, a level at which he was already competent and had won, he seemed to feel more happy and developed in confidence and physique. With Stunning, it was all about making him as comfortable as possible, especially as he was an older horse with considerable mileage on the clock. All the work paid off at Kentucky in 2002, when we got our four-star placing. Since then, he has been amazingly consistent, winning a stream of events including the British Open title at Gatcombe in 2003.

We were selected for the 2001 European Championship, which heaped on the pressure for Stunning, especially as we were in the fourth slot. When Leslie Law and Shear H_2O made a mistake in the water, it meant we had to go clear and I can honestly say that waiting for my turn was one of the worst eventing days of my life – all I could think was 'Oh God, of all the horses to be on.' Stunning was always aware when the stakes were high and would respond accordingly, his confidence vanishing. I still feel that his clear round that day was one of his major achievements.

Of those three horses, Steadfast had the attitude, Chaka the scope and Stunning the speed. In contrast, probably the easiest horses I've ridden are Frank Andrew's Cosmopolitan, whom I took to the Atlanta Olympics, Moon Man (easiest of all) and Mary Guinness's Tamarillo and, arguably, I have learned less from them. And, proving the fact that the most unlikely horses can be successful, in theory, of these three only Cosmo could be considered an ideal event horse.

The Leicestershire dealer Vere Phillipps obtained Moon Man from a trekking centre in Ireland. He was brought to England to be sold as a hunter. However, he wouldn't settle – Vere gave up trying after hunting him 10 times in 20 days – and even now he will go mad in a prize-giving. I bought him for what I saw over the stable door: he reminded me of Steadfast and I thought he looked kind, but when he came outside he looked fairly average but I enjoyed riding him. He was seriously raw material, but he's a grafter and has been a very rewarding lesson in how trainable a horse can be if he's willing to learn; Moon Man had to be taught how to move, gallop and jump, but he's a genuine uncomplicated horse whose brain and conformation have eventually allowed him to do everything very easily.

If Moon Man is the worker, Tam is the playboy, or perhaps they are the carthorse and the china doll. Tam looks more like a seahorse than an event horse and the thought of eventing him was a joke to begin with. Apart from being obviously talented with incredible paces and jumping ability, there was nothing to suggest that he would make an eventer: he had a spooky, suspicious nature, was particularly untrusting and didn't have a great desire to be trained – he was rather like thistledown floating around in the wind. But when I rode him, I felt that I just had to try with him; I couldn't let him pass me by. Tam has a unique athleticism – he's more athletic than all the horses I've ridden put together. You never feel the ground beneath him; he can sail through a bog making the ground feel like the fairway on a golf course and, over time, he has learnt to work with me and he has developed trust. He was second at Badminton in 2002 and I feel there is more to come from him, as well as my other horses. I now have a better string of horses than ever before, including two French-bred ones, and I'm really looking forward to the future.

Finally...

It is often said that in order to succeed at eventing you need a bit of money, a bit more talent – and an awful lot of luck. Eventing is both a physical and mental challenge; when you're feeling discouraged, it's worth remembering that there really are plenty of rewards for the work. Otherwise it wouldn't attract the number of competitors and followers – none of us would be there if we didn't love it.

Cavalcade striding confidently through the water at Gatcombe.

Career file

1985 8th Junior National Championships
22nd Junior European Championships
(Steadfast)

1987 5th Junior National Championships
Individual silver, Junior European
Championships (Steadfast)

1988 4th and team gold, Young Rider European
Championships (Steadfast)

1989 Completed Badminton
Individual bronze and team gold, Young Rider
European Championships (Steadfast)

1990 3rd Young Rider National Championships
(Faerie Sovereign)
Team gold, Young Rider European
Championships (Steadfast)

1991 19th Badminton (Steadfast)
1st Windsor (Thomastown)
10th Bramham (Uncle Sam II)
10th Boekelo (Steadfast)

1993 7th Badminton (Chaka)
Team member, European Championships
(Chaka)

1994 Completed Badminton (Chaka)
7th Punchestown (Thomastown)
2nd Scottish Open Championships
(Chaka)
2nd British Open Championships (Chaka)
1st Burghley (Chaka)

1995 1st Bramham (Cosmopolitan II)
1st British Open Championships (Chaka)
1st Scottish Open Championships (Chaka)
6th Blenheim (Loch Alan)
6th and team gold, European Open
Championships (Cosmopolitan II)
5th Boekelo (Faerie Diadem)
No 1 National (British Eventing) rankings

1996 6th Bramham (Lismore Lord Charles)
Member of 5th placed British team at
Olympic Games, Atlanta
Completed Burghley (Loch Alan)
5th Boekelo (Mostly Mischief)

1997 3rd Badminton (Cosmopolitan II)

1997 1st and 5th Blarney Castle (Pie In The Sky II
and Mulligan's Shenanigans)
1st British Intermediate Championships
(Mr Beluga)
2nd Scottish Open Championships
(Cosmopolitan II)
Individual bronze and team gold, European
Open Championships (Cosmopolitan II)

1998 1st Necarne Castle, N Ireland (Moon Man)

1999 3rd Chantilly (Western Reef)
7th Bramham (Moon Man)
4th Eventer's Grand Prix, Hickstead
(Western Reef)
2nd Achselschwang (Moon Man)

2000 1st Compiègne (Western Reef)
1st Blarney Castle (Tamarillo)
1st British Open Championships (Moon Man)
1st British Intermediate Championships
(Tamarillo)
1st and 2nd Blenheim (Stunning and
Tamarillo)

2001 1st Burgie (Highland Lad)

2001   1st Lummen (Western Reef)

1st Sandillon (Western Reef)

2nd, 3rd, 5th and 6th Scottish Open
Championships (Stunning, Springleaze
Macaroo, Moon Man and Tamarillo)

1st and 2nd Scarvagh, N Ireland
(Western Reef and Barclay Square)

9th and 13th Burghley (Moon Man and
Springleaze Macaroo)

2nd, 4th and 9th Windsor (The
Professor, Highland Spirit and Diable
Au Corps)

6th and team gold, European
Championships (Stunning)

No 1 in National (British Eventing) rankings

2002   4th Lexington, Kentucky (Stunning)

2nd Badminton (Tamarillo)

1st Burgie (Ballincoola)

6th and 8th Bramham (Highland Lad and
Just A Sovereign)

3rd and 4th British Open Championships
(Moon Man and Stunning)

1st and 7th Burghley (Highland Lad and
Moon Man)

Team bronze, World Equestrian Games
(Tamarillo)

No 1 in both National (British Eventing)
and World (FEI) rankings

2003   3rd Kentucky (Moon Man)

22nd Badminton (Highland Lad)

1st Chatsworth (Stunning)

7th Saumur (Coastal Ties)

1st and 2nd Bramham (Ballincoola and
Wallow)

1st and 2nd British Open Championships
(Stunning and Moon Man)

1st British Intermediate Championships
(Tom Cruise)

1st Luhmuhlen (Tom Cruise)

Team gold, European Championships
(Moon Man)

1st Boekelo (Tom Cruise)

5th and 8th Le Lion d'Angers (Ildalgo
and Igor de Cluis)

No 1 in National (British Eventing)
and No 2 in World (FEI) rankings

Flatwork

I admit that I find dressage the least inspiring of the disciplines, but I still believe it is an essential element and integral part of all phases. A well-trained horse that is capable of performing dressage movements well will not only be more competitive, but will be a much more enjoyable ride, whatever you plan to do with him; he will also be a safer ride.

It is more important to have a horse with a great temperament, than one which is overly talented. The ordinary, trainable horse with a reasonable level of ability can often surprise both rider and trainer, and progress beyond all expectations. If the training is carried out correctly from the beginning, without missing any steps or cutting any corners, and the basics are established to ensure the horse listens to and respects his rider, the rider's life in both producing and riding the event horse will be made infinitely easier. A horse must also be encouraged, even in his flatwork, to think for himself.

To achieve respect, I believe that horses must be disciplined in a fair way, but never dominated; it can be a fine line between the two, and some horses need more discipline than others, but a horse that is over-dominated and submissive in the dressage might well not think for himself across country.

What is required of the horse?

A young horse needs to understand the boundaries in which he has to perform, therefore you must be quick to reward a good piece of work; I feel that a horse is much more likely to remember what to do through reward than by being punished or ignored. Horses perform to please, they don't do it to avoid reprimand – there are people who do train on the latter basis, but it doesn't ultimately lead to success. To me, it's an important principle that the horse is willing to perform without having to be dominated.

In order for the horse to continue enjoying his work, it's also important that he's not over-trained: variety is crucial in maintaining that enjoyment and keeping his spirits up.

It's important to reward your horse as soon as he does something right. Reward, not reprimand, is the best way to teach horses.

Even hacking is part of the whole basic training, as is all the work he does out of the school. Therefore, when on a hack remember to make him work properly and keep him swinging forward, as this is where he will learn to go forwards and think for himself.

The dressage test

The basic aim in a novice dressage test is for the horse to walk, trot and canter when asked to do so. The judge will be looking for him to show energy and forwardness, to stay in a rhythm without being hurried, to stay straight, maintain a consistent outline and perform transitions obediently. The judge will expect to see a difference in the strides but will not expect fantastic lengthening or a mature outline – these are all things that come with practice and establishment over the years.

The requirements in the untrained horse are a good walk and canter – the trot can be improved – and a willing outlook. Moon Man is a good example of a horse who has extremely ordinary natural dressage ability but who benefits from having a great attitude towards work. As a three-year-old, he had been a trekking horse in County Sligo, carrying 17-stone men, but from the first time I rode him, I could tell that he had galloping and jumping ability and a great temperament, which was the selling point. I felt that if his body could be improved, his mind would certainly allow it. It took a lot of time to do this, and was a matter of developing his strength and suppleness through work. It was worth it however; although he has never turned into a flamboyant or extravagant horse, he has produced some very good marks, which proves what you can do with a trainable horse.

While the ideal horse has natural flowing paces, excessive movement can be just as much of a disadvantage as poor movement. Flashy movers can be difficult to train; their balance and rhythm is often easily lost, and they can be more prone to injury. In eventing, there is a lot to be said for the economical horse, who doesn't take so much out of himself. Don't be lured by an amazing mover, because often the disappointing reality is that it can't jump or doesn't find jumping easy.

For someone starting out in eventing, much is gained by having a schoolmaster horse, as I did. However stiff or unglamorous such a horse may seem, they can teach you plenty. While it is everyone's dream to grow up with a young horse, the reality is that inexperienced riders rarely know enough to make the partnership work.

As a young horse, Moon Man had only ordinary dressage ability but his good mental attitude has enabled him to learn to produce a good test.

FLATWORK TIPS

■ Even if you don't enjoy flatwork, it is excellent for improving your horse's jumping skills

■ Instantly reward good work in a youngster

■ Forwardness and freedom in every pace goes a long way towards achieving good work

■ Flashy movement is not necessarily a good thing in a potential dressage horse

■ Your position is crucial to your horse's performance – make sure you are sitting correctly

■ Work on having a secure but elastic contact, allowing the horse's energy to come through from behind

■ In every training session make time to work long and low

The rider's position

The fundamental point about the dressage position is that the rider must have independent balance and must not be relying on the horse. Technically, to achieve balance sitting in the saddle, there should be a perpendicular line from shoulder to hip to heel: the rider who is in balance will neither be gripping with their hands or with their legs. When teaching I always ask myself this question: if I were to remove the horse from under the pupil, could he or she stand on the ground in that position without falling over? That is, are they sitting with weight evenly distributed, demonstrating that they are not relying on the horse? The rider's position has great influence on a horse's performance; while some top riders have succeeded with raw talent and, perhaps, an unconventional position, a correct seat undoubtedly goes a long way to optimizing your prospects of success. The principles of position that I have been trained to work with are: to keep opening your inside shoulder to allow the horse to come round with his shoulder, to keep your weight very slightly to the inside, and always to look in the direction in which you're going.

If you sit in the right position then you're well on the way to having the horse going forward. A seat that is behind the centre of balance will produce discomfort in the horse's back and resistance in the mouth, while if you tip forward, it is fundamentally difficult to have your horse connected from leg and seat into the rein.

When working on your lower body position, make sure your knee is relaxed so that your lower leg can come into contact with the horse. A tense and gripping knee results in a tendency to draw the leg back or away from the horse, therefore losing its effectiveness. For the upper body, it is important for your head to be sitting comfortably

When the rider relies on her hands to make the horse put his head in the right position, the result might look correct at the front end but it does little to encourage him to work from behind.

For a horse to be able to work well there needs to be a relaxed straight line from the rider's elbow to the horse's mouth and a good balance from his shoulders, through his hips, down to his heels.

on your shoulders and for your shoulders to be relaxed – not hunched and tense, which is a common fault. Consider the shape of your shoulders – a rounded shoulder is a tense shoulder. The tension will be transmitted down your arms to a solid hand with no give, which will result in mouth resistance. An insecure position like this means you have to rely on your hands to maintain an outline. This might, ultimately, convince the horse to put his head in the right position, but you could not say that he is working from behind or through his body. A good exercise to relax your shoulders is to shrink your head down into your collar and move it gently from side to side, which in turn relaxes the spine.

Crookedness is another handicap to the horse, and for riders of any level, someone watching their position from the ground can be essential in correcting any crookedness or bad habits that tend to creep in.

Contact

Contact between the horse's mouth and the rider's hand should be secure but elastic, allowing the horse freedom and comfort but maintaining the energy created by the leg. The concept of contact was explained to me at a young age by an elderly Polish colonel, who had taught my mother. At the time I thought it was quite boring; this endless balancing on the reins from one degree of contact to another seemed miles from reality – and I longed to go off galloping! Once I started riding more seriously, however, it wasn't long before I realized how crucial it was. You will never make any progress in getting a horse to go better until you learn to ride forward from the leg into the hand.

Not only must the rider's position be in balance but it must also be straight, above left, with a relaxed even pressure.

The rider on the right is crooked and out of sync with her horse. This is causing discomfort to both her and the horse, and will result in the horse performing poorly and not going forward.

Far left: The aim is to have a relaxed but straight line of contact between the horse's mouth and the rider's elbow, as here.

Left: Rounded shoulders and low hands are common rider faults. Along with these two faults, this rider also has her lower leg too far back, this makes her unable to connect the horse from behind and into the rein.

The paces

The most important thing for any rider getting on any horse is to establish forward-ness and freedom in every pace. From a young age, horses must be encouraged to accept the rein and take it forwards and down, and as part of their development, they will learn increased engagement and self-carriage.

From my long-term train Sheila Cotter, I have learnt the importance of working the horse long and low. This stretches and loosens muscles before you start to work, so it acts as the warm-up part of the training session. It also teaches a horse to stretch his head and neck, and therefore maintain balance by stepping under himself and develops hindquarter strength and a good topline. I believe that by starting a session in this relaxing manner I am less likely to come across tension in the horse during his work.

Walk

The horse should always march forward at the walk with plenty of swing – it generally follows that a horse which walks well can also gallop. In all the walks – free, medium and extended – there should be maximum overtrack, which means that the horse's hind foot should step well in front of where his front foot was placed.

In free walk on a loose rein, as here, the rider has very little contact with the horse's mouth. I like the poll to stretch lower than the wither and the nose to be beyond the vertical with the horse taking the rein forwards. I also look for a maximum overtrack of the hind legs. A long rein is not a loose rein – there is still a contact between the hand and the mouth – many people don't appreciate this difference, and it can lose you points in a dressage test.

In medium walk the horse's whole frame becomes compact – the outline is rounder and his neck is shorter. However, it is still important that the contact is maintained and that his nose doesn't come behind the vertical.

The horse's outline in extended walk is shorter than it is in free walk on a long rein. The poll has to be at least slightly higher than the wither and the head position is on the vertical. Maximum overtrack and a swing in the walk is still required.

Trot

In trot, the same principles apply as in walk. I look for a horse to swing through his back, working from behind into an elastic contact.

When I first go into trot, I encourage the horse to stretch down, taking my hand forwards and loosening his muscles and relaxing before the training session starts.

Once the horse has warmed up, it is important to establish a correct working trot. Here, Archangel, a six-year-old intermediate horse, steps forwards from behind into the rider's hand and takes a forward working trot in a correct outline. It is important that this outline and stride length is maintained when the rider goes into sitting trot.

Canter

I want a springy three-beat time in canter. For cross country, I look for a ground-covering stride and for dressage and show jumping, a bouncy powerful stride. As in trot, when warming up in canter I encourage the horse to stretch. Once he can canter in balance, I introduce counter canter (cantering on the 'wrong' leg). initially by looping off the outside track (see pp.44–5). When he does this is in a good balance, I work increasingly in counter canter which is a great way to improve a horse's overall canter strength.

When I first start canter work I take my weight out of the saddle allowing the horse as much freedom as possible and encouraging him to produce a forward stride. Once his back is thoroughly warm and relaxed, I then start to concentrate on more collected work sitting in the saddle.

The important thing to achieve is a canter with energy, therefore encouraging the horse to step under himself. Here, a good level of engagement can be seen with the horse's leg coming under the rider.

Gaining balance and outline

During a trot to walk transition encourage your horse to go forwards into the downward transition rather than shuffling into it with several shorter trot and walk strides. It is also important that he stays up in his balance and does not fall on to his forehand. Although this horse has at times become a little short in the neck, he has maintained a good balance throughout and his first two walk strides (right) have a good long, positive step.

A trot, halt, trot transition with the horse staying in balance throughout the downward transition. The end result – an unsquare halt – is not perfect, but this is because the horse came slightly against the hand as he stopped, which is typical with a youngster.

For a trot to canter strike-off transition, the horse needs to be balanced and soft in his trot before he is asked to canter so that the transition is as smooth as possible. This is a smooth transition but the horse does lift his head slightly, showing that he is not yet sufficiently engaged behind. At this stage, it is not something of great concern: he is a young horse and this will improve with training.

Riding the horse in different shapes and at different paces will improve his balance, outline, straightness and suppleness, and prevent him becoming one-sided, all of which are just as important in preparing him for the jumping phases as for doing dressage tests. Work to achieve these includes riding circles, squares, half circles, serpentines, as well as change of rein, figures of eight and transitions – so the horse learns to react to the rider's leg and go forward as well as come back into the hand – and lateral work, including leg-yielding and shoulder-in. Transitions, reinback, counter canter and polework are also extremely useful in improving a horse's balance, suppleness, reaction to the aids and overall manoeuvrability.

As you ask for bend, your shoulders must follow the horse, allowing him to come around. It is also important to have a secure inside leg, as here, to keep the horse bending all the way from poll to tail, rather than just in the neck.

From behind, it is clear how important the rider's outside leg is in supporting the horse through the bend and preventing his quarters from swinging out.

On turns in bends and circles, it is important that a horse goes forward by working through from behind, and that the rider looks ahead. I like to keep in mind the principle that the horse's body should be curved on the exact line of the circle being ridden, which means that a horse on a 20-metre circle will be less curved in his body than one on a 10-metre circle.

In a walk to canter transition, before asking for the canter strike-off, it is important to collect the walk so that you get the horse's attention. This horse shows good engagement as he strikes off into canter, but his expression reveals that he is confused by what is being asked, and although he goes into canter, there is a resistance. To improve on the roundness in the upward transition, I would train him on a smaller circle.

Horse and rider straightness is crucial, whatever the phase, and should be a point of concentration from the beginning. A crooked rider (left) will make a crooked horse. It is useful to have someone on the ground observing both horse and rider, as it can be difficult to feel whether you are straight when you're on board.

Leg-yielding is a useful suppling exercise and helps to teach the horse the basic principle of moving from inside leg to outside hand. Here we are leg-yielding from right to left so the horse moves from my right leg to my left rein. The contact in the left rein must remain secure and the horse's left shoulder must be controlled by my left leg. As the movement progresses, the angle of the yield increases and the limbs cross over well.

Shoulder-in is one of the hardest lateral movements to ride and requires a horse to be on three tracks. As I begin the shoulder-in to the left, I ask the horse to come off the track with his outside shoulder, placing his off-fore on the same line as his near-hind. This angle needs to be maintained throughout the shoulder-in movement. It is important that the horse bends evenly through his body and neck.

In this half-pass to the left, we move sideways, staying parallel to the outside of the arena. Cross-over of hind and forelegs is rhythmical and equal and the horse bends in the direction he is going without losing the quality of his trot. My right leg is moving the horse across and my left leg is keeping the forward movement, while my hands have positioned the horse's head and neck into the correct bend.

Introduce reinback at a relatively young age, regardless of what you plan to do with your horse. It increases his manoeuvrability and is a very useful general movement – invaluable when you are opening gates for instance. Train him to go backwards primarily from a leg and body aid; hand aids must be minimal. Here, I have put my leg back and slightly softened in my seat, allowing the horse to come up in his back and move backwards. The legs must move back in a two-time rhythm.

If your horse resists the reinback aid, as here, stop asking, re-establish his outline and ask again. If the result is the same, find someone to stand on the ground and help push him back. The reinback is easy to teach, but some horses can develop a mental block about it, which can be troublesome in a dressage test.

Right: In counter canter it is usual to keep the horse's bend of body and neck slightly towards his leading leg. Sometimes, as an additional exercise, I bend the horse the other way in order to work on his suppleness and canter quality

Below right: The flying change is crucial for jumping so it should be introduced early in your horse's training – irrespective of the level of dressage you are doing. Flying changes enable a horse to maintain flow and balance while changing direction on a show-jumping course.

Polework

TRAINING TACTICS

■ Vary your routine for each session to keep your horse interested in what he is doing. Put the poles on a circle or at angles to each other, for example

■ Be quick to reward good work, especially in youngsters as this tells them when they have done the right thing

■ With a horse that tends to rush at everything, use a grid or row of poles to force him to think about what he is doing with his feet and slow him up

■ Canter work over evenly spaced poles soon shows up any inconsistency in stride. Count each stride to help maintain a rhythm

I use work over poles on the ground to teach a horse balance, co-ordination and self-carriage, as well as to encourage him to flex his hocks and pick up his front feet, making him concentrate on where they are going to land. Training over poles will also increase muscle tone and flexibility. In young horses, it helps them to find and maintain a constant rhythm in all the paces, too. Place them about 1.2–1.3m (4–4½ft) apart for a 16 hh horse. Obviously the exact spacing will depend on the stride of your horse, but he should be able to trot over them with an even stride, his feet landing midway between each pair of poles.

Riders can benefit from polework, too. It is especially useful in teaching you to maintain a rhythm in trot and improving your sense of balance, ensuring you do not rely on the reins; you must be prepared to allow your horse to go forward freely and to move his head and neck, without losing the contact.

Providing variety

Poles can be used to create obstacles that can be trotted over (or cantered over in a more advanced horse) to increase athleticism and suppleness as well as to ensure the horse is listening to the rider rather than doing his own thing. They provide interest and a new dimension in training sessions, which can otherwise sometimes prove rather dull to the young horse. Like all other aspects of flatwork, it has a purpose beyond schooling, in that it is gearing the horse for the jumping phases to come.

I favour thicker poles, like telegraph poles, as they are heavy and don't roll about as easily when hit. This teaches the horse to respect them and to make more of an effort to avoid touching them, which will have a knock-on effect when he comes to learn to jump – this is particularly important with horses that are very bold or inclined to be sloppy. Their slightly bigger size makes a horse work that bit harder, too. My poles are also shorter than most and this teaches both horse and rider the importance of being straight, something that comes in particularly useful when jumping narrow fences.

In the sequence the horse is initially working rather short and you can see this in the second photograph, where he has both front feet inside one pair of poles. However, I encourage him to stretch out with a bit more confidence and by the end of the row of poles he is placing his front feet and his back feet more evenly in the middle of each pair. You can see that he lifts up his legs well, making sure that his feet clear the poles. This will also increase his muscle tone and flexibility.

William favours these thicker poles as they encourage the horse to get the feel for poles that don't move when they are knocked.

The real thing
Riding a dressage test in competition

Prepare

The most important thing about riding a dressage test in competition is to be well-prepared. Firstly, this means learning the test properly, because you won't concentrate if you're worrying about remembering it. Practise riding it at home, from start to finish, but don't do it too often, otherwise your horse will begin to anticipate the next movement and may rush.

Warm-up

Secondly, organize your warm-up so that you neither overwork your horse, nor run out of time and become flustered. Collect your thoughts so that you always enter the arena in a positive frame of mind, even if your warm-up hasn't gone as well you might have hoped. Visualize yourself showing your horse off, feel proud and ride him as though he's the best horse in the world.

Ride positively

One of the most common causes of a disappointing dressage performance is the rider not riding forward through the test because they are not feeling positive. You often see a horse warm-up beautifully and then produce a mediocre performance due to their nervous rider merely sitting through the test instead of riding through it. A confident rider position will always secure a few extra marks so, as nervous as you might be, try to look confident and secure in your position. This is why the top riders get the marks they do; they are rising above a horse's lack of talent and putting on a show. Even on a tense horse that feels as if he might explode, it is far more productive to ride an attacking test than just to be passive. Any judge faced with the exhausting task of assessing 40 tests in a day would much rather see a bravely ridden test speckled with errors than a lacklustre, overcautious performance.

Here I am looking ahead to the next movement. Looking ahead is instrumental in positive, accurate and forward riding.

Aim for accuracy

Next to riding positively, your most important aim is to be accurate. Accuracy is entirely your responsibility, and is a common area in which marks can be gained or lost, regardless of the horse's ability and paces.

There is no getting away from the fact that, unlike the jumping phases, dressage is subjective. Therefore, you should work on emphasizing your horse's strengths and playing down his weaknesses. For instance, if you know he has a particularly good trot, ask him for the maximum in this. Don't focus on the fact that, for example, he resists halt or won't stand still; you will only make it an issue and cause tension. Instead focus on, perhaps, his extended trot, and getting the maximum out of that. It is better to accept a mark of 5 or 6 for the halt and work on getting an 8 or a 9 for the trot, than to develop a fixation about something that your horse finds difficult, which could result in lower marks across the board.

When you know your horse does a movement well, make sure you really go for it. Judges are always impressed by a rider that has a crack at it.

Make sure you do your transitions at the designated letter as inaccuracy is the easiest way to lose marks and is entirely the fault of the rider.

AT THE COMPETITION

- Keep a positive mental attitude and ride positively, even if things aren't going too well. There is nothing to be lost from riding confidently, and everything to be gained

- Emphasize your horse's skills and play down areas in which he is less talented

- Imagine yourself as the judge and give a performance to hold their interest

Jumping

For me, the most important aim of jumping training is to teach the horse to think for himself so that he becomes capable of jumping a fence on his own initiative. This is crucial in cross-country where a horse that waits to be told exactly what to do is not a safe or enjoyable ride.

Working over coloured poles at home is a great introduction to cross-country training. You can build all kinds of patterns at various distances on a flat surface where your horse is unlikely to hurt or frighten himself, and where, if you plan it properly, he will also enjoy himself. To begin with, I educate a horse to jump loose or on the lunge, so he learns naturally without help or interference from a rider. I'm not a fan of using trotting or placing poles at this stage, unless the horse seems to be having exceptional trouble judging his stride. I simply start with a pole on the ground and this is eventually replaced by a small obstacle. I do a lot of work with crosspoles as they are excellent for ensuring that the horse learns to jump straight.

Focus points

The main points of focus during the early stages of jumping training are straightness and rhythm of approach, working towards a controlled and relaxed jump. If I am not achieving these qualities in a young horse's jumping, I then introduce placing poles before and after the fence to encourage him to look what he is doing and keep in a rhythm.

It is important for the young horse to learn to jump out of both trot and canter, but this process does not require big fences: at the early stage of training, height is irrelevant. When the rider is introduced to the horse's back, the horse must still be encouraged to think for himself; I find the best way to do this is to stay in trot until he is completely confident in choosing his own take-off point.

Once a horse is jumping a small fence happily, I introduce combinations and a small course of fences, making sure I keep the work light-hearted and avoiding the temptation to over-jump. A tired or overfaced horse can frighten himself and he may discover that stopping is an option. If each step is taken carefully and thoroughly and no stage is missed in the early training, then he is far more likely to develop a depth of confidence and enjoyment that will always stand him in good stead in future.

JUMPING TIPS

■ Develop your horse's ability to jump on his own initiative by jumping him loose when you start his training

■ Use crosspoles to produce a straight jump

■ Placing poles help a horse to keep a rhythm, but I would try not to use them unless they are really necessary

■ Make sure your youngster learns to jump out of trot before canter

■ Never overface a young horse, and make sure his jumping training is fun

■ Keep a bold horse interested in his work by varying the jumps and what you are asking him to do

■ Produce confidence in a spooky horse by regular repetition and keeping progress slow

Developing technique

It doesn't take long to assess the amount of natural talent your young horse has for jumping, and any problems that require attention will become evident equally quickly. I hope to see an athletic ability combined with an instinctive reaction and aptitude for adjusting to each obstacle, as well a willing attitude toward jumping. If a horse has these qualities, then his natural technique over a fence can be developed more easily. With a cautious horse, it is important to take each day slowly and to repeat exercises regularly, whereas with a bold horse, I tend to change the question being asked to keep him on his toes and to prevent him becoming more confident than he is already. Again, this doesn't need to be done through raising the height of fences, but more through varying the exercises. Grids, with varying distances, fences jumped off turns and figures of eight, and simple whole courses will keep the horse's interest and teach him to react to whatever is in front of him.

So much of cross-country is to do with adjusting speeds and strides, and jumping knock-down fences in the school is all part of the training. Another aspect of cross-country is accuracy, as there is an ever-increasing tendency among course builders to make narrow fences and tricky lines, with the emphasis being on obedience and honesty in the horse. You can simulate these in the school – arrowheads, corners and narrow fences – and use guiding poles initially so that the horse gets the idea of staying straight.

Correcting faults

It is in the early stages that a horse's jumping habits become established – with care, good technique can be instilled from the start. If your horse is awkward over jumps perhaps with dangling legs and a hollow back, this is the time when improvement can be made. Simple gymnastic exercises, such as a grid of fences in which bounce distances are varied with one- or two-stride distances, will teach a young horse to assess what's in front of him and how to adjust his jump, picking up his feet and rounding his back, to clear the fences.

As I mentioned earlier, the basics of cross-country begin with jumping poles in the school or field. If, at this stage, your horse shows a tendency to lack respect for fences, I recommend taking off his leg protection when you jump fixed fences, the idea hopefully being to teach him to respect what he is jumping. The more he learns that fences fall down and the less bothered by this he becomes, the more casual he will be in his attitude to jumping.

A typical fault that develops in the exuberant young horse is rushing fences. With a horse that shows this type of keenness, it is important to jump him regularly on a little-and-often basis. Stay in trot for as long as possible when approaching the fence, and work on jumping small fences on circles and figures of eight so that he is not approaching them on a straight line (rushing is always more likely on a straight line); remember, however, to keep the horse's body straight over such fences. The idea is to use repetition to convince him that jumping isn't something to get excited about.

The type of fences I jump at home depends on the individual horse. If I have a bold and forward-going horse, I do not jump too many fillers and imposing-looking fences in training. I believe that when he does get to a competition he'll have much more to look at and will jump with more respect for the fences. However, with a spooky horse, I practise over fillers and colourful fences at home in the hope that when he gets into the competition ring he will be less surprised by the appearance of the fences.

If you have a horse that jumps well at home and at the practice fence and then tenses up the moment he goes in the arena, it is obvious that he is lacking match practice. In this case, take the time to compete him more regularly in straightforward show-jumping competitions so he gets used to the atmosphere in the arena.

This horse is neither forming a good shape over the fence, nor picking up his legs. There are many exercises to help improve a horse's jump; gridwork and gymnastic exercises are particularly useful in increasing suppleness and developing strength. Introduce poles on the ground or leaning against the fence to keep the horse straight.

Using grids

This basic double of crosspoles with no placing poles is a simple exercise to keep the horse straight and is useful as a stepping stone to a more complex grid (bottom). The crosspole itself can help the horse to make a good shape when jumping.

A grid of bounce crosspoles is designed to keep the horse straight over his jumps. Any deviation from the line needs to be corrected by the rider opening the necessary rein. The crosspoles encourage the horse to stay central to the jump and make him tidy with his front legs.

The stride-bounce-stride grid complex is a simple exercise for teaching a horse to lengthen and shorten his frame over a fence, to think for himself and to learn to distinguish a stride pattern. The horse should enter and leave the grid in the same rhythm; a horse with a tendency to gain ground might require placing poles between the stride fences to keep his stride pattern regular.

Left: The exercise over crosspoles has translated in straightness at a competition over an obstacle that has no artificial means of keeping the horse straight. Many horses have a natural tendency to jump to one side, so a good training in straightness is crucial.

Introducing fences

The wide variety of fences that will be met both in show jumping and on cross-country courses need to be introduced, in simple form, at an early stage in your horse's training. Many types of fences, such as ditches, are fairly easy to re-produce in the school at home and establishing confidence over these will make subsequent cross-country schooling, as well as the transition to competition, much smoother.

I have positioned a simple water tray between two uprights for this horse's introduction to a ditch. His reaction is typical – one of complete surprise. Although he doesn't refuse, he is not convinced that it's at all safe to go over and gives the water feet to spare. It is important to allow a youngster plenty of freedom so that he is not punished in such a situation by the rider being left behind.

The exercise should be repeated until he approaches calmly and jumps it normally.

The next stage is to place a rail on top of the water tray. This is a similar principle to jumping a trakehner, although you will not be going at the same speed. The idea is for you to ride the fence as though the water tray is not there.

Once a horse is trained and confident over ditches at home and when schooling, a ditch like this should pose no problem at all.

Angles and accuracy

Once your horse has learned to jump confidently in straight lines, he needs to be schooled to jump corners, fences at an angle and narrow fences without wings. As well as increasing his ability to judge a jump and think about what he is doing with his legs, this will also gradually get him used to the idea that he can and should tackle whatever is put in front of him, whether it is a corner, an arrowhead or a narrow jump into space. For the rider, the challenge is to keep the horse straight, as the approach on an angle or to a narrow fence offers the opportunity, and temptation, to run out.

Here, two simple show jumps are positioned a stride apart and at an angle. With this type of schooling, increase the angles the jumps are set at as your horse becomes more comfortable with the task.

This is a variation on the theme: here the horse is being asked to turn on the approach and then stay on a straight line. He is slightly crooked at the first fence, tending to lean right, but he is quickly corrected with the right leg and left hand and jumps the second part of the combination in the required straight line.

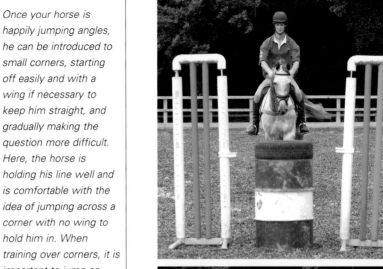

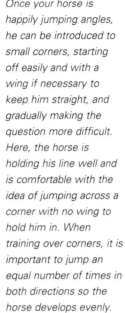

Once your horse is happily jumping angles, he can be introduced to small corners, starting off easily and with a wing if necessary to keep him straight, and gradually making the question more difficult. Here, the horse is holding his line well and is comfortable with the idea of jumping across a corner with no wing to hold him in. When training over corners, it is important to jump an equal number of times in both directions so the horse develops evenly.

When introducing your horse to narrow fences, I recommend starting off with wings, so preventing him from learning that he can run out. As he becomes confident and competent, remove the wings. This simple barrel is not something I would expect to jump without wings until the horse had reached an advanced stage.

Riding a show-jumping track

- Always walk the course

- Think of the course as a whole, not a series of individual jumps

- Look out for unexpected challenges such as awkward cambers and distractions outside the arena

- Keep the warm-up to a minimum and don't panic if you knock over the odd warm-up fence. Most horses jump better in the ring

- Ride the course according to your horse's experience and react quickly to the feel he is giving you in the arena

My first piece of advice is: walk the course. This sounds incredibly obvious, but while every rider automatically takes the time to walk the cross-country course, they often don't pay the same respect to the show-jumping course. Riders arriving at a competition after the jumping has started find that they can't get onto the course, so they have to manage by watching other rounds. While it is important to watch how the course is riding, this should not be taken as a substitute for actually walking it yourself. There are usually course-walking breaks during the day, and I strongly recommend you seize such opportunities. It is also worth asking a more experienced rider if there is anything you should be looking out for.

In a competition situation, it's easy to ride a course by just going from one fence to the next, without thinking about how you're doing it. Just as you would before a cross-country course (see pp.142–143), visualize the show-jumping track as a whole. Take a few moments to go over in your mind how you're going to ride your turns and approach the fences, this is especially important if you are riding a green or inexperienced horse that will be having to cope with the demands of competition atmosphere.

Even in the lower levels of eventing, there will always be some related distances and combinations and, while each horse has a different stride pattern, it is an advantage to know how a distance walks for the average-striding horse. If you know the distance, you can make necessary adjustments for your own horse.

Things to look out for when walking the course include any awkward cambers, which might cause a horse to lose his balance – not all courses are as flat as you might wish – and slippery turns where you need to make sure you have him gathered together. Look out for fences placed near the collecting ring, which might cause him to be reluctant, backward-looking or nappy, or those that involve jumping towards spectators, banners or things that might spoil his concentration. On entering the ring on a green horse, I do my best to trot past as many of the spooky fences as possible to help him to become accustomed to the situation.

During your round it is important continually to assess how your horse is going and whether or not he is coping with the course. If his eyes are out on stalks and he feels tense, take a little bit more time between fences and even bring him back into trot to give him the opportunity to strike-off on the correct lead, allowing him the best chance of being balanced and relaxed. Don't worry initially about the odd time fault. On the other hand, if he is coping with the questions, then I recommend that you use flying changes between relevant fences, so teaching him to maintain rhythm, self-carriage and impulsion.

Warming up

The warm-up for the show-jumping phase need not be a long drawn out process and, in many cases, six practice fences will be all your horse needs. Remember that the aim when warming up is to save your best jumps for when you are in the arena. I once had a horse that I never warmed up because if I caught him by surprise, he would concentrate harder and the chances of him jumping a few fences clear was higher. Many horses are like this.

I use a practice fence simply for warming and stretching my horse's jumping muscles and sharpening his reactions and for testing how reactive he feels. If he jumps well, there is no need to go on and I am very often happy to go into the ring having knocked down a practice fence, hoping that he might concentrate harder as a result.

My typical warm-up is as follows: a couple of crosspoles jumped out of trot, followed by a couple of small verticals in canter, then a small parallel, followed by a big parallel.

In some instances, I go from a big parallel back to a maximum height vertical before entering the arena. While encouraging the horse to jump well, I would not assist him in any way. If you only jump six or seven fences, the odd repetition is not going to result in a horse being over-jumped before going into the ring.

You don't necessarily need to jump a big fence in the warm-up. It is more important that your horse is jumping in a relaxed manner, staying on a straight line and respecting his fences.

In show jumping, uprights are frequently jumped badly by event horses who do not achieve enough shape over them. Such fences need to be jumped with power rather than pace, and the rider should avoid using too much hand on take off as this may result in the horse knocking down the fence. Gentle support from the hand should also be sufficient to ensure a horse is not clumsy with his front legs.

This parallel is approached slightly uphill. The canter is weak on the approach and the fence is jumped too flat and without sufficient impulsion, the horse knocking down the back rail with his hind legs – a good indicator that the canter lacked power and engagement.

Cross Country

For me, cross country is what it's all about, and it is meant to be fun. The most important rules to remember for cross-country preparation are: that the horse must understand that he has to look after and think for himself – from this he will ultimately learn to look after his rider, too, and will be a safer and more enjoyable ride. Most horses love going across country and want to please; if they don't, it often means that something has gone wrong in their training, either to cause them to lose confidence or to allow them to realize that stopping is an option.

The teaching process

It is crucial that the teaching process is gradual and thorough. In the early stages, the horse must be given time to assess what he is being asked to jump; initial jumping lessons should be over small fences and out of trot so that he can see where he should be putting his legs. If a horse gets used to jumping at speed right from the start, he will not fully understand what he has jumped, which is unsafe, particularly when it comes to bigger or more complex jumps.

I was brought up, as were many of my fellow riders, to view a refusal as a sin, and it was more than my life was worth to return home having had one. I am a strong believer that this should be the key principle in any rider's approach to cross country. The desire to avoid a refusal makes the rider want to get to the other side of the fence and that positive thought will be conveyed to the horse and will encourage the rider to use his legs.

My other strong belief, which is closely linked to the first, is that a young horse should be introduced to more complicated fences through having a lead from a more experienced horse. Having a lead gives a horse huge encouragement and makes him less likely to consider stopping. This is also a good reason for starting with small

TRAINING TACTICS

Warm-up is a crucial part of the training session. During warm-up, encourage your horse to start listening to your aids, and work on his rhythm, balance and straightness. It is important that your stirrups are short enough for you to be able to balance securely in canter, giving the horse's back plenty of clearance. Cantering with your weight off his back is more comfortable for him and helps him to loosen his muscles and relax.

This horse is having second thoughts about dropping into the water but forward motion is maintained by strong use of the leg accompanied by a firm whack. While you should react quickly when you can feel that your horse is considering stopping, generally you should never ask him to jump higher than knee height from a standstill as this can cause a fall.

fences, because if a horse does hesitate he can be urged on to jump from a standstill without any danger to himself or the rider, thus reinforcing the idea of keeping going.

Of equal importance to both these beliefs is my conviction that the horse should associate going across country with having fun. Always reward him with a pat when he has jumped a fence well in training to let him know that you are pleased with him.If he is allowed to become tired, either mentally or physically, or to lose confidence by being over-faced, he will remember the experience. Little and often is the key, as is finishing on a good note, such as over a fence the horse finds easy.

Once they are established, horses will need less practice – my advanced horses probably have a couple of schooling sessions a year, while young horses might have one before each competition – but it is important for the rider to keep up with the training. This is difficult if you are a one-horse rider, but try to maintain the momentum by jumping something regularly, attending cross-country clinics and supplementing eventing outings with hunter trials or small shows. Looking for things to jump or negotiate while out hacking – small logs, banks, ditches – is a good idea but I recommend that you only do this when you have company. In fact, a rider should never jump when they are on their own.

POINTERS TO SUCCESSFUL CROSS COUNTRY

■ React to how your horse is feeling, rather than having an inflexible plan in your mind as to what is going to happen. Be prepared to adapt your schooling session – or cross-country round – to accommodate how your horse is performing.

■ Develop a feel for when a horse needs to repeat a fence to achieve a more confidence-building jump (a similar principle to knowing when your horse has done enough). The rider must be quick to pick up on any loss of confidence.

■ If a horse loses confidence with, for instance, a bad landing in water, don't be afraid to re-start the exercise and regain the horse's trust; go back a stage and walk and trot into the water rather than expecting the horse to launch himself in again. The principle is to leave a happy impression in the horse's mind, even it means not achieving as much as might have been hoped.

■ From the start, train your horse to go straight; keeping him between your hand and leg at all times which will, in turn, give him the confidence to go where you want him to go.

■ Don't let the horse get in the habit of stopping. While it might sound basic to mention using your legs, lack of leg use is the single most common fault found in cross-country riding because the desire for the rider to take the leg off approaching the fence is natural.

■ In training, while it is important to jump individual fences in a relaxed way with plenty of breaks in between, it is also important to establish a horse's rhythm and balance, which means not continually stopping and starting. Having warmed up over single fences, then put a small course together of five to ten obstacles and keep the horse moving throughout.

■ There is a difference between the horse being active and being fast; it is important at all times to ride with a forward, positive approach, which has nothing to do with speed. By doing this, the horse learns to find his own rhythm, and the rider learns how much or how little time each individual horse needs in front of the different types of fences.

Position

Fundamental to a good cross-country position is a secure lower leg. Without this, it is impossible for you to establish a still upper body, at the same time looking ahead and maintaining a constant contact, allowing your horse the freedom to make the best jump possible.

Cross-country schooling is the perfect time for you to concentrate on your position. While each rider has their own style, balance and security are of paramount importance to everyone and, for me, these are attained by riding with my stirrup leathers anything from two to four holes shorter than for show jumping. There are various arguments about length of leg, and I can see that there is an element of individual preference – riders like Lorna Clark and Karen Dixon have had considerable success with a longer leg position – but I support a short length. It comes down to physics: a bent leg or arm has much more strength than a straight leg or arm. I believe that the bent leg better supports the rider's body securely above the saddle and gives it

Allowing the horse freedom to use himself over the jump comes from the rider having a good cross-country position

Moving the upper body forwards keeps the rider central to the horse's balance

balance. The rider is then in a better position to help the horse and has less need to hang on to the reins for balance. Also, the shorter length provides a more secure and still lower leg, which will prevent the rider getting in front of the horse's movement and will enable them to balance above the saddle when galloping between fences, so giving the horse's back freedom. There is nothing worse than seeing a rider's back-side slapping in the saddle between fences while they hang on to the reins to keep themselves upright.

Upper body stillness and looking ahead are vital for balance

Lower leg security is paramount if you are to achieve a strong cross-country position

Constant contact gives the horse confidence on take-off

Contact

The other vital ingredient for confidence across country is contact. In fact establishing the right contact with the horse's mouth is one of the most demanding aspects of cross-country riding. Too much contact is restrictive and will cause a horse to be backward thinking. Some horses actually stop because their riders have not given them enough freedom: the horse becomes confused and thinks he is obeying a command to stop. The opposite to being restrictive is losing contact altogether (known as dropping the horse) and this is the most common cause of a stop or error because it takes away the horse's security, leaving him with no direction, especially at the time of take-off. Put simply, the horse just doesn't know what to do.

Slipping the reins

Dropping the horse should not be confused with slipping the reins, which is a skill and a vital part of cross-country riding. The horse's main tool of balance is his head and neck and if he cannot have the freedom to use these, he will find it difficult to balance on landing, particularly over a drop. Slipping your reins means opening your fingers to allow a longer length of rein; it does not mean altering your position. On landing you should recover slipped reins as quickly as possible.

This is an example of a horse being 'dropped' in front of a fence. The horse emerges into the light and sees the next fence; the rider has allowed the reins to become too long, and has adopted a defensive position. On the stride before take-off, contact has clearly gone and the rider has moved forwards, leaving her horse with no security. This results in his loss of confidence and decision not to take off.

Here a supportive contact is maintained right up until the horse has taken off, the rider softening in time to allow the horse to use himself over the fence. This position gives the horse all the necessary confidence and support so that he is not even thinking about stopping. Although many riders do get away with riding on a loose rein, especially if they have a genuine horse, on an inexperienced or ungenuine horse, it is vital that contact is maintained at the point of take-off.

Banks and Steps

Banks and steps are a test of a horse's athletic ability and judgement, which means that the approach must allow the horse time to assess what is being asked of him. In the rider they highlight the importance of lower leg security, which is why course designers have begun to place fences at the top and bottom of banks and steps to catch out those riders who are not in correct balance. These types of jump are some of the most difficult to negotiate while remaining in position, but it is vital because if you are too far forward or too far back in the saddle, your horse will have to work much harder.

APPROACH AND POSITION

- Approach with controlled power, not speed, thus providing sufficient impetus to take on the uphill leap ahead.
- So that he can balance, give your horse freedom in his head and neck both when you are going up and when you are coming down, but do this without losing contact.
- Avoid being over-anxious on the jump up. By trying to help the horse, you risk getting in front of the movement, which will make him go flat and long and might lead to tripping.
- Be ready for the possibility of a big jump up, making you get behind the movement. This in turn will make it more difficult for the horse to lift his back end on to the bank and, once there, may mean he loses impulsion.
- Aim to bring your shoulders upright above the horse but release your arms forwards as you would when jumping fences on an uphill slope; horses usually find these easy, but they do need impulsion.

A simple log on a bank teaches the horse to maintain balance on approach, while giving him time to think about where he is going. The rider needs to have an independent balance and instil confidence in the horse through the leg and a supportive yet allowing hand. The angle in the rider's arm reflects the amount of rein given at each stage.

This narrow bank complex is useful for training a horse to keep going, keep straight and to look where his feet are. He approaches slightly off line, but is soon corrected. The rider is in balance throughout and, coming off the bank, he slips the reins to allow the horse more freedom. However, contact is retained so avoiding a peck on landing.

This sequence clearly shows the effort required to jump three steps up and emphasizes the importance of an approach of controlled power. Horse and rider are maintaining a good balance, which has enabled them to get to the top with plenty of impetus. Again, contact is constant, providing security and straightness, but the horse is being given sufficient freedom to use his entire body for this big effort. It's important that the rider does not restrict the horse when jumping such a fence.

Below: The rider is allowing her horse the same freedom to jump the same type of fence, but this is in an advanced competition. Ideally, her reins should be slightly shorter throughout, but her lower leg is secure and the horse is jumping confidently and keeping straight.

Coming off a bank complex, this experienced combination is in good balance. However, the rider's shoulders are a fraction too far forwards, which might have caused problems had there been a subsequent fence.

Below: Although this rider's position looks a little stiff, he has retained balance over this steep downhill log, keeping his shoulders back.

Below: Despite being at the back of the saddle with long reins, this rider is giving his horse support from the leg. However, at the next element he goes to the other extreme, losing all security and tipping well in front of his horse's balance.

This combination (above) gives a great impression of power and energy. Both horse and rider are straight, making the negotiation of this fence as easy as possible. Straightness at this type of fence is harder to achieve than you might think, as can be seen in the sequence on the right where the horse is bent to the left and the rider is tipping to the right throughout. While the fence is successfully negotiated this time, this is the type of detail that riders should concentrate on in training as it could easily allow a run out (here to the right).

Many horses in this Eventer's Grand Prix at Hickstead had never seen such a bank as this, meaning they had to assess it in seconds before jumping. There is no definite edge and it can be read by the horse in different ways. Some gallop straight at it, not registering the steepness and others have been known to try to jump straight over, not appreciating the size. Here the rider is in good balance, giving the horse time to see what is ahead, keeping her shoulders well back should he do anything unexpected. Her lower leg is spot on, encouraging him forwards.

The horse's balance is crucial at a downhill fence. Here the horse is having a look at this unusual obstacle – his head has come up and he is thinking about backing off – however he is well-balanced and sufficiently on his hocks to jump it. He is slightly hollow over the fence, but when the landing is downhill horses do not need to be encouraged to bascule as this may encourage them to over-jump.

Over the same jump this rider is being defensive, protecting the horse from the fence with her hand and ensuring a hollow but safe jumping style. As the rider develops confidence and allows a bit more with the rein, this horse will learn to lower his head.

Below: The difficulty in this type of complex is to maintain a horse's straightness and forwardness while keeping a good balance in order to tackle the very narrow fifth element at the bottom. Here, the horse is straight and, although the rider has perhaps slipped the reins too much coming down the steps, there is a consistent contact, even though the hands have come up too high in an attempt to maintain that contact. A reasonable balance and the security given to the horse has ensured there is no deviation from the line, which results in a successful jump of the final element.

Right: This willing horse is not receiving much guidance from his pilot, who is out of balance with an insecure lower leg. Although balance is retrieved at the second step down, the reins are still too long. The horse is being ridden in a hackamore, perhaps indicating he prefers to be left alone, but if he did decide to deviate from his line, with that length of rein and lack of contact there would be little the rider could do to correct him.

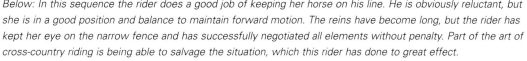

Below: In this sequence the rider does a good job of keeping her horse on his line. He is obviously reluctant, but she is in a good position and balance to maintain forward motion. The reins have become long, but the rider has kept her eye on the narrow fence and has successfully negotiated all elements without penalty. Part of the art of cross-country riding is being able to salvage the situation, which this rider has done to great effect.

Drops

Drops are simple to ride but it is possible to make silly mistakes at them, mainly due to the rider losing contact with the horse. Again, your balance is critical because your horse must have freedom to move while you retain the contact. The idea is to keep his front end as light as possible, as you would when jumping fences on a downhill slope.

APPROACH AND POSITION

- Make your approach with enough impulsion and commitment to avoid a stop – even a moment's hesitation will be penalized. However, don't go too fast as this will make your horse over-jump and peck or fall (right), which could cause loss of confidence and even injury.
- Ride straight at a drop. Riding at an angle could result in a fall if your horse loses a leg.
- To maintain your balance, make sure you are sitting in the centre of gravity as you come down; slip the reins enough to allow your horse some freedom in his neck but keep the contact to prevent him losing direction.
- If you choose a more forward position (as some riders do), you must have an incredibly secure lower leg.

Above: A variety of seats are used to jump this hedge. From left to right: the old-fashioned hunting seat (although not classical as she is leaning too far back) is effective as a horse in this shape is unlikely to trip on landing; the next rider has a good position, but her leg is too far back for real security, with the toe down, and the horse looks as though he might land on his forehand; in the third example the horse is landing in a good balance with the rider adopting the safety seat and slipping his reins, though he is a little stiff and, again, slightly too far back. Far right: this rider is doing his best to retrieve an awkward jump in which he has allowed the horse too much freedom so that he lands on his forehand. He sticks his arm out to retain his balance. I get the impression that if the horse pecked, the rider might fall off, as he is not straight in the saddle.

Below: The drop at Le Lion d'Angers is a daunting complex for a young horse as it is among trees and surrounded by people, and involves a drop on to the road followed by an angled palisade on to a slope. However, the drop is clearly visible, which means horses are less likely to falter on landing. Here, the rider has slipped the reins, but has maintained a contact throughout. Having dropped off the 'house', the rider has given the horse support to enable him to jump the final element without loss of balance.

Right: This inexperienced horse has over-jumped this hedge, where the drop was invisible and unexpected, and he pecks on landing because the approach was too fast. However, the rider has stayed in balance and has maintained contact, giving the horse every chance of recovery and encouraging him to pick himself up. If the rider had been further forward, the horse could have fallen over.

Horse and rider are out of balance. The descent is too speedy and the horse is on his forehand. If you look at his near hind it is clear that he has slipped, partly contributing to the loss of balance. Such banks need to be tackled in a controlled and balanced canter, with the horse's weight firmly on his hindquarters.

Above: Here the horse is dropping down sensibly and economically, resulting in a maintained balance, which will make any following fence easier to jump.

Right: A secure lower leg is essential here, where there is a drop into water, as horses can lose their footing and peck on landing. Horse and rider are landing in balance and are looking ahead to the exit.

Into space

With a fence where neither you nor the horse can see the landing, you need to ride with total commitment in order to give your horse the confidence and impetus to take off into space. Into space fences are always testing and it is common for an inexperienced or less confident horse to lower his hindquarters defensively as he jumps, which can result in the rider being unseated.

APPROACH AND POSITION

- Plan an active approach; it should not be too fast, but must have plenty of energy with a good contact to the point of take-off.
- Keep your position secure and upright as you must be ready for the horse to falter. This is physics again – sitting upright provides more strength than leaning forward or back.

The perfect jump – horse and rider are in total harmony and balance over this into-space type fence, which is approached via a ramp. The horse is jumping confidently because the approach has been calm and without fuss; the rider is sitting still and quietly, maintaining contact but allowing the horse to land gently.

This is a slightly uncomfortable jump. Perhaps the rider has not been sure what the horse will do and has gone into an excessively defensive position. He has launched himself into space and has lost the horse's back end on landing. However, the rider quickly gets himself back in balance and is well able to help the horse to continue.

These sequences show three distinct styles over the same fence.

Above: This horse appears to have jumped carefully and slowly, but the rider begins to look worried surprisingly early, his lower leg slipping back, and he has started to 'hail a cab'. The landing shows a good retrieval of the situation, but as the pair moves on he seems to be balancing himself on the horse's mouth.

Centre: Although this pair looks initially promising, the rider then reveals a lack of security in her position and has tipped in front of the point of balance. Had her horse pecked, she might have suffered an annoying, and avoidable, rider fall.

Below: Perfect harmony, with the rider already looking ahead on landing (although, to be critical, she is slightly ahead of the movement) picking up her horse and saving valuable seconds with a quick getaway from the fence.

Trakehners and ditches

While some horses appear never to notice a ditch, for others they can be a major worry. In fact ditches and trakehners are merely straightforward fences designed to look awesome and be 'rider-frighteners', which means the rider's attitude is crucial. This is a typical example of a fence where the strength of the contact can imbue confidence in the horse, and along with giving good leg aids will ensure your horse jumps with no worries. Instinct often compels riders to over-attack ditches but to have the reins looping, which serves only to frighten the horse.

APPROACH AND POSITION

- Treat a ditch or trakehner as a triple bar – as if the ditch weren't there – and approach at a decent speed and with commitment.
- Keep your leg firmly on and maintain a secure contact.

Introduce young horses to ditches in trot so they get the chance to look at what they are expected to jump. The rider's leg must be on firmly, encouraging the horse to keep going and jump calmly without ballooning. This is the type of fence that a horse can safely jump from a standstill (top) and the rider must be prepared to follow an awkward jump. It is important that once the horse does take off, the rider gives him freedom, ensuring a comfortable experience. A horse that doesn't take to jumping ditches straight away is not necessarily a bad horse, so don't be disheartened. It is a strong instinct for horses to be suspicious of holes in the ground.

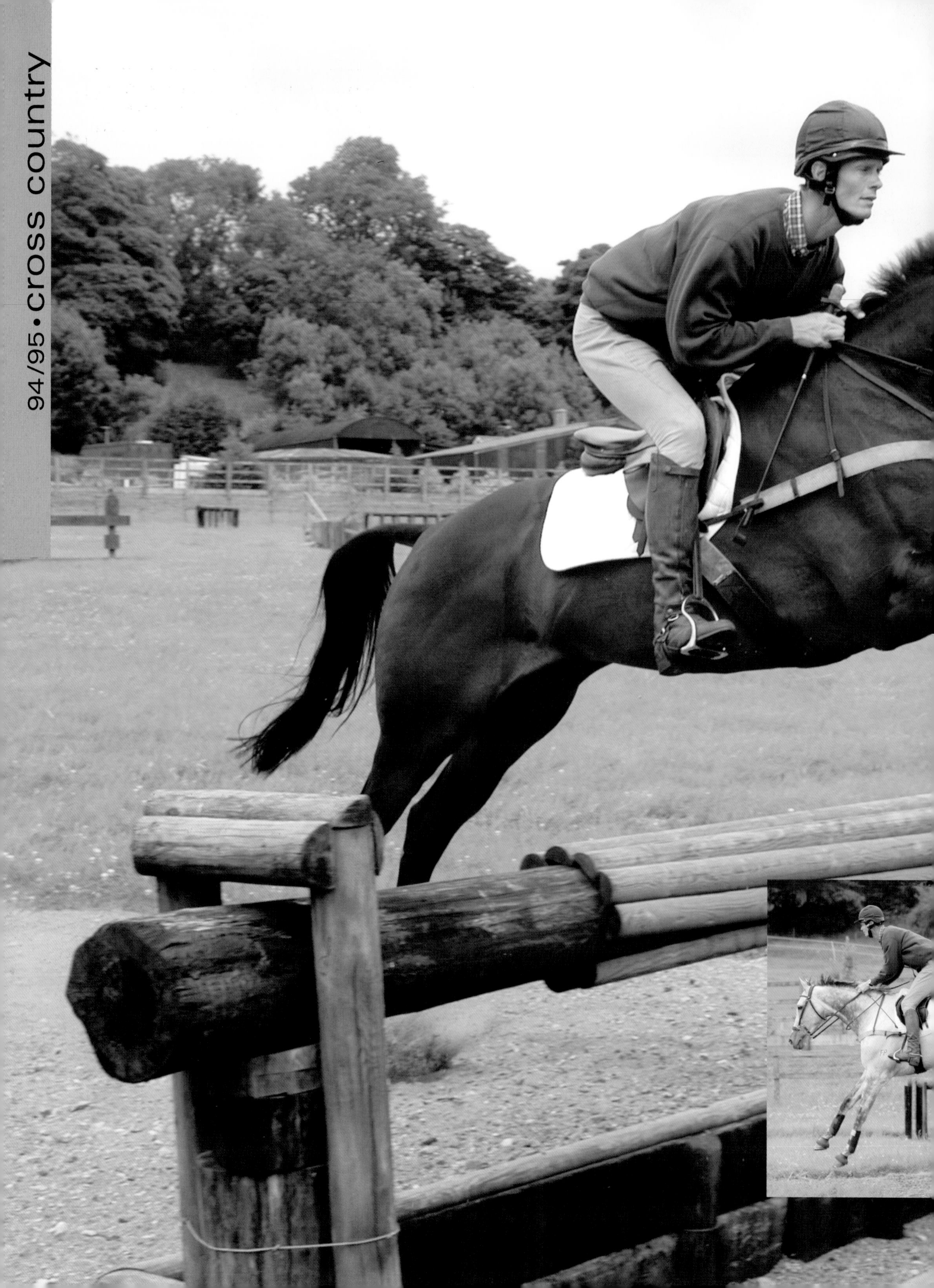

An illustration of the maxim that the rider should never look down, always ahead, so that the horse treats a trakehner as a normal fence. I was always taught that if you look into a ditch, you'll end up in it!

TRAINING TACTICS

One horse I had was worried about ditches – negotiating Centaur's Leap at Burghley on Loch Alan was not funny – and he would back off when he thought a ditch was coming. This made me ride him even more strongly, but the main thing I had to do was to keep hold of the contact. In Loch Alan's case, the strength of the approach was irrelevant, it was the strength of the leg supported by a secure contact that gave him confidence.

Even though this horse is wearing a hackamore (he had a mouth ulcer at the time), I am still maintaining contact with him as he looks at the ditch and lowers his body on approach.

Accuracy fences

Jumping narrow fences with no wings is a good way to train your horse to be accurate from the start.

The term 'accuracy fence' covers arrowheads, pimples, angles, corners, bounces and related distances. These have all become more popular over recent years with course designers seeking to test the rider's technique and eye for a line. It's not just about the way you ride the approach, but these fences also need to be walked carefully. The aim is to achieve the line that is most obvious for the horse to understand. Alternatives should also be inspected because if, for instance, your horse's confidence has been shaken at a previous fence, you may feel it sensible to switch plans and go for a less demanding route. If you have planned and prepared properly, you need not waste too much time with an alternative route, should it become necessary.

APPROACH AND POSITION

- Spend time preparing and balancing your horse on the approach. In most cases he will need to be in an engaged, balanced and steady canter, between hand and leg and going straight. By having him firmly under control, you minimize the risk of a glance-off.
- Use a slightly wider hand to ensure maximum straightness. Hands that are closer together can be less effective. Think of your horse being held firmly in a channel between your hand and leg so that he has to follow the route you request.
- With your horse between hand and leg you can keep him moving straight, or fluently through turns
- Make sure you look ahead to where you want to go.

Below: As is often the case, this introduction to a line of three narrow fences doesn't go immediately to plan. From the beginning the horse begins to drift to his right; despite the rider having plenty of notice, he is rather slow to correct the situation, eventually opening the left rein on landing after the second element! With correction from the right leg and left rein, the horse comes back on to his line and jumps the third element happily.

In order to train your horse to jump accuracy fences, I recommend using a series of guidance poles positioned on either side of a narrow fence (above) gradually taking them away one at a time (right) so that you eventually jump the fence on its own (opposite). The training process is a bit like the old gymkhana game of barrel elimination, but instead it is done over years.

Above: In a narrow triple, such as this double of brush fences, the approach needs to be one of complete control with the horse between hand and leg, giving him no option to run out.
Do not attempt narrow fences without wings until your horse is already showing considerable confidence in what he is being asked.

Left: At this arrowhead, which is jumped off rising ground, the rider is doing a good job of keeping the horse straight, signalling clearly to him by opening her hand to the right and applying her left leg (centre). This gives him all the help he needs to clear the fence.

On the approach to the same fence the first rider (top right) keeps her horse well-connected between hand and leg, ensuring a clean jump, while the second rider (right) has dropped the contact and left her horse to sort himself out, which he generously does, despite skidding. She has, however, allowed him freedom of his head and neck so that he can correct himself. Although the rider is back in a good balance on landing.

TRAINING TACTICS

The training for riding related distances and combinations across country is no different to that for show jumping. The key is to have balance between fences, which is achieved by teaching the horse to maintain a consistent speed and rhythm. The distances at related fences and combinations need to be walked carefully so the rider is prepared and can plan at what speed to approach the fence.

This rider has an excellent secure seat, giving the impression that her balance wouldn't alter whatever the horse did beneath her. She conveys the stillness that a rider should aim for when jumping a fence of this nature. The less the rider moves about, the easier it is for the horse to do what is required.

A straightforward stride-bounce combination over two logs provides a useful exercise in teaching a horse to lengthen and then shorten his stride and to judge a distance for himself. Rounded logs encourage a good jump and are more forgiving than rails should the horse make a mistake.

The brush construction of this double means it can be approached at a decent speed. However, a bullfinch can encourage a very big jump, which may result in the distance between the two becoming very short. For an experienced horse, such as Stunning, this fence should not present much of a problem.

Above and below: At first glance, these two rider styles look similar, but there are some differences. On approach, the top horse is thinking about his rider more than the fence and is showing anxiety, whereas the coloured horse below looks relaxed and is approaching in an ideal balance. At the point of take-off, the second rider's balance has gone slightly ahead of the movement and he has lost his lower leg. Although he regains this quickly, his positions through the sequence indicate more body movement.

TRAINING TACTICS

Bounce fences should be introduced to horses from a young age in the school so that by the time they meet them on a cross-country course they will be familiar with the question. The bounce needs to be approached in a short active canter that gives the horse every chance to be prepared for this test of athleticism. As with all jumping, the rider should sit as still as possible so as not to unbalance the horse and yet allow him the freedom to use himself to achieve a comfortable jump

Above: This horse has become unbalanced through the turn to the bounce and, as a result, he has never really locked on to the question ahead. The rider is doing a good job of keeping him between hand and leg, however, so giving him confidence. In the middle of the bounce, he has to correct the horse to keep him straight; the resulting jump shows a near loss of balance for the horse, who is being helped by his jockey to stay on his feet. Throughout, the rider's secure lower leg position ensures he is never in danger of losing his balance and, despite the horse's wavering, there is never any likelihood of a run-out.

Left: In contrast, this horse is totally focused, ears pricked, on the bounce ahead. He remains straight and balanced throughout, and the rider is able to make an economical turn, which will save time. However, his lower leg position is not ideal: it drifts back to start with and later slips quite far forward, though his upper body position does not appear to move.

Lucinda Green shows why she is the best-known cross-country rider of all time with a perfect execution of this double of corners at Blenheim. She has set up the horse perfectly for the combination, maintaining contact and a secure position so that in the unlikely event of anything going wrong, she is instantly in a position to save the situation. Notice how little the upper body has moved in this sequence.

Right: This double of corners is on a camber with a curving related distance, and calls for complete accuracy. The pair appears to jump the first corner too quickly, which forces the rider to pull sharply to regain control for the three strides to the second, enabling the horse to jump in the right place. Though the rider is in front of the movement on take-off, she maintains contact and keeps the horse straight. Here it could well be argued that the martingale is helping to correct the horse's head position in order for him to be able to focus on the fence.

This pair produces a more controlled jump over the first corner and lands in a better balance. Even though some adjustments need to be made (centre), the three strides come up easily and a good jump over the second corner is guaranteed. Note the total commitment shown by horse and rider in looking ahead to the second element.

These two 'houses' have been placed on an extreme angled distance but the rider has managed to keep a straight line throughout. She appears to have organized her attack and set herself up positively, without considering any deviation, and made quite a good job of maintaining contact. She does, however, show a tendency to get in front of the movement over a fence but there is a feeling of confidence and determination about the pair and the horse is enjoying himself.

This combination contains many factors: it is approached on rising ground on to a road, up a bank, on a related distance to a narrow triple brush. The horse has jumped in well and calmly and has taken a confident first stride across the road with his sights set firmly on the brush. However, when the rider asks him to adjust his stride, there is resistance. This is a common reaction in youngsters and the rider must soften his hand so that the horse can concentrate on what is ahead and yet not lose the contact at the point of take-off as this could result in a run-out. Here, the rider's leg has gone back slightly, but his upper body has remained still and in balance.

Water

TRAINING TACTICS

The introduction of water in a horse's training must be done gradually so the youngster realizes there is nothing to be frightened of. Make sure you have a lead horse available to help because you may need to persevere until he goes in. It is likely to store up long-term trouble if you have to end a session without getting him in.

There is always an element of unpredictability about how a horse will jump into and land in water, and you need to be ready to react to a peck or an over-enthusiastic leap, often produced by a green or less confident animal. More than at any other fence, it is important for you to pick up on any feeling of uncertainty, even if the horse doesn't actually say 'no'. Often riders do nothing about their horse's confidence until they have a stop, but in fact they should react to a mistake every time. If a horse I am riding has a fright in water in competition, I will re-school him before the next event. Always approach steps out of water with control and respect as they can be difficult and hazardous – give your horse the chance to judge the distance without hurrying.

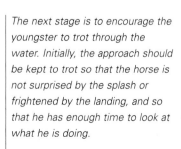

Young horses need to get used to the feeling of being in water and I always encourage them to have a drink and a splash. This helps them to become relaxed with the concept and learn that it can be fun.

The next stage is to encourage the youngster to trot through the water. Initially, the approach should be kept to trot so that the horse is not surprised by the splash or frightened by the landing, and so that he has enough time to look at what he is doing.

APPROACH AND POSITION

- In competition, approach water at a strong yet short canter. Give your horse time to assess what is being asked but don't reduce speed so much that he grinds to a halt.
- Maintain a short, bouncy canter while travelling through water because it will make it easier to judge how to jump an obstacle in the water or one out of it.
- Avoid allowing your horse to fall into a long, fast canter stride – the cause of many mistakes. Make sure he doesn't become strung out and laboured in his stride.
- Unless your horse still finds cantering in water too difficult, trot is not advisable as it makes tripping out over a step more likely.
- An obstacle sited in water needs plenty of preparation, even if it is a straightforward fence in itself. Allow your horse time to find his feet and judge the jump through the spray while maintaining maximum impulsion.
- Sit up and maintain hand and leg contact throughout.

Move on to dropping off a bank into water, do this first in trot and when you are convinced your horse is ready, approach in canter. Be prepared for excessive enthusiasm or hesitation and be ready to react to either.

Survival seems to have been the key as far as rider position is concerned, but the horse is very happy! He has been exuberant from the beginning and has then taken a big green leap into the water, landing on all four feet. His legs are all over the place, as are the rider's, but the horse is showing commendable enthusiasm to finish the job. The only saving grace is the rider has maintained lower leg security.

TRAINING TACTICS

The way a horse jumps into water can reveal that training has been insufficient – appropriate training will teach him that there is nothing to be frightened of. However, some horses need more practice than others; I always made sure that Stunning went into water in between events, even though he was experienced, because his confidence was boosted by regular schooling sessions.

Just to prove I can cope with water! Here, the horse makes a balanced and controlled approach and the consistency of my leg ensures a neat jump. The horse lands in balance.

The training exercise practised earlier (p.114–15) appears to have paid off with this tidy and confident jump into water in a competition. The horse is more relaxed with what he is being asked to do and the rider is able to go with him and maintain a better balance.

Banks out of water are among of the most problematic of fences and tripping is a common fault. This is because horses have difficulty in judging where to take off out of water. Here, three horse and rider combinations clearly show the effort that is required in managing this type of jump while making the distance to a following fence: the first horse (below left) could easily have done another stride on the bank; the second one (opposite) has taken off too soon and has only just made the bank but the rider has maintained a good balance, while the third (bottom) has made the best job. Her horse has come gently to the bank and has jumped up easily.

Right: The rider is doing his best to keep this horse in canter – it would like to trot – and the resulting jump in water is ungainly. The rider position is good over the fence and on landing, where he has opened his fingers to slip the reins. Although the reins do become too long, the rider manages to maintain the necessary contact to help the horse out of the complex.

Below: Here the canter has got somewhat long but the rider has given his horse the confidence to get a good jump over the log and achieve a balanced landing.

Above: Here, as the horse and rider exit the water they are required to make a turn to meet the next element of the fence. The horse is unprepared for this and stops. The rider has not ridden the roll top strongly enough, has tipped forward and dropped the reins. A more generous horse might have helped her out, but here her faults have cost her a stop.

Left: The next pair make a better job, with the rider driving the horse forward. Although the her legs have drifted back, she is using them, and she has sufficient rein contact on take-off.

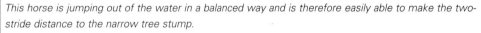

This horse is jumping out of the water in a balanced way and is therefore easily able to make the two-stride distance to the narrow tree stump.

A bounce into water is considered the ultimate in water-jump difficulty. The fact that the obstacle is a bounce means that the rider is unable to come to the fence too quickly and strongly, which they might prefer to do if their horse lacks courage. The horse needs to be given time to assess the bounce question, but there also needs to be sufficient impulsion to get him into the water.

Above: This rider sits well back during a big jump into water. Having slipped her reins, she is quickly shortening them again and is therefore able to help the horse regain its balance, despite the extravagant jump, and jump out of the water in an organized fashion. Her lower leg has remained still and, while her reins have become longer, she is maintaining a contact.

Left: In comparison, this pair has not managed as well; the horse is out of balance and the rider has got left behind and is not able to help the horse to get a good jump out up the step. He subsequently opts for the long route, but if that choice were not available, he might have got into trouble at the narrow final element of this complex.

Coffins/sunken roads

The key to these fences is in the approach, because it is that which will determine how the remainder is jumped. Too slow an approach will result in a lack of impulsion and possibly a stop because the horse is always on the back foot; too fast an approach and the horse isn't able to judge the question, which can result in a fall.

APPROACH AND POSITION

- Maintain a strong, bouncy canter and provide plenty of energy and commitment, along with a secure rein.
- The steeper the approach to the ditch element, the more important it is to approach in control – spend more time in the preparation.
- Hold your position and contact at the point of take-off: it is crucial not to drop the reins and flop forward.
- Having got in successfully over the first element, remember to keep your leg on, maintain contact and really ride through the remainder of the complex.

Left: A young horse being introduced to a coffin in trot. He has to learn to judge the rail in while also looking ahead at what is to follow. Things do not go entirely according to plan here; he focuses more on the ditch than the first element, resulting in a leg being left behind on the rail (this is why training fences should be small). He then spooks at the ditch and produces another chaotic jump. There was improvement on the repeat performance.

Below: This sunken road follows the same principle as a coffin: the horse is being asked to judge a rail before the main part of the fence. Again, a young horse would naturally focus more on the sunken road and could easily make a mistake at the insignificant rail. Here, Moonstone is judging what is ahead effectively and showing a good balance throughout.

The horse looks unbalanced on take off and screws over the first element, nearly landing on his nose. He then almost falls into the sunken road and eventually fails to get enough impulsion to jump the last element. The rider loses her balance and the pair do well not to have a fall. She then doesn't get her balance back quickly enough in order to be able to help the horse tackle the bank out to a narrow arrowhead. The approach could well have been too fast and the line might have been dubious. Throughout this sequence the horse has received very little direction from his rider, which proves how important it is for the horse to be able to think for himself.

Above: This is a good example of what can go wrong in a coffin combination, and this horse and rider have made a good job of retrieving the situation. The horse was clearly concentrating on the ditch ahead and so leaves a leg behind on the rail coming in. The rider subsequently loses her balance and gets in front of the movement and the resulting jump over the ditch happens more by good luck than good judgement. The horse has jumped violently left over the ditch and the rider does well to turn him back on track towards the third element. She has been saved by a secure lower leg.

Left: In contrast, this combination has jumped the coffin with apparent ease. The rider is in balance from beginning to end, giving the horse every opportunity to make a good job of the fences and ditch. He barely moves in the saddle and the contact remains constant throughout.

This pair approaches the sunken road at Blenheim with a powerful but controlled canter in which the horse's hocks are well underneath him. The rider moves the horse up to the fence and gets a good first jump into the complex. He then sits back in preparation for the drop down on to the road. Even though the distance across the road part is short, the rider is all the while pushing the horse on to ensure he achieves the long distance to the last element.

This is a variation on the coffin theme with water in the middle, and the rider in the top sequence shows how it should be done. He approaches in a controlled, balanced canter, allowing the horse the chance to see what is ahead. The pair jump through the complex calmly, making it look easy. The horse in the bottom sequence also jumps in well but becomes unbalanced – almost stopping in the water. He finds it difficult to regain balance, particularly as he has no help from the rider, and there is not enough control to jump out. Too late, the rider tries to correct the situation by shortening her reins, but her efforts are in vain, and the horse runs out.

Spooky fences

Obstacles such as owl holes, roofed fences or jumps from light to dark or dark to light are all potentially spooky for horses. There is now a trend among course designers, particularly at advanced level, to try to create unusually sited fences. These obstacles are usually straight-forward in themselves with an insignificant measure of difficulty, it is their presentation and situation that can be distracting. However, they need not always be a problem – when a horse's blood is up and he is running across country, it is often surprising what he will happily take on, but they do need practising, especially those with roofs as many horses will duck the first few times they go through. This is because they feel restricted and it is usually something they become more comfortable with.

APPROACH AND POSITION

- A horse's eyes take longer than ours to adjust when going from one degree of light to another, hence when jumping from light into dark, or vice versa, give him time to assess the fence while keeping him moving.
- Be prepared to ride strongly and with utmost commitment to prevent your horse losing his nerve at a spooky fence.

Hanging logs and fences on rising ground can unnerve a horse because it isn't clear where they need to take off. It is most important that they don't take off too early. Here the rider is encouraging the horse forward with firm riding and a softening hand into the fence and asking him to take off nearer the base of the fence to achieve an easier jump.

Potentially spooky fences need plenty of practice, especially those with roofs (far left), which tend to make horses duck – they need to learn that they will not hit their heads. A horse that has reached the level of Burghley (right) will take this sort of fence in its stride. This horse is focused on his job and has not even noticed that he is jumping through a summer house.

Right and below: Fences going from light to dark are one of the most challenging questions for a horse, not least because their eyes take longer than ours to adjust. An additional problem here is that this fence, the third on the Gatcombe course, is followed by a drop, giving the horse no idea where he can expect to land. The approach, should be ridden with plenty of impulsion to give the horse confidence.

Sensing her mount's reluctance, the rider of the grey horse commits the cardinal sin of tipping forwards and flapping her reins in the hope that he might jump. He stops at the jump with the rider obviously in front of the movement and lucky to escape falling off. While the horse below is also having a good look, the rider has kept her body in balance and given the horse a secure contact. In so doing, she has given him confidence to jump the fence, despite her balance tipping forwards at the point of take-off.

Below: Fences from dark into light are less complicated, as horses will always naturally see light as being an opening. It looks like this rider's stirrups are too long, which may be a reason for his loose lower leg, which in turn has caused slightly too much upper body movement.

Riding to speed

I learned to ride to speed simply by riding courses at a pace at which I felt comfortable and then seeing how I got on – nothing more scientific than that! When you see your results, you can tell whether you were going too fast or too slowly and this should help you develop a feel.

Speeds can be practised at home by measuring out a distance around the edge of a field and checking your progress with a stopwatch. By all means do this, but don't become preoccupied with it, for there is no better place to practise than at a competition. However, it is not an exact science, especially as different events are measured more tightly or more leniently. One reason why stopwatches are banned at novice level is to get less experienced riders to learn to judge speed by feel rather than on the button.

One of the secrets of riding to time is to achieve a constant rhythm. This doesn't mean going flat out, because then you will waste time trying to slow up in front of

This sequence shows a horse jumping at speed and making a quick, smooth getaway from the fence. The horse has been ridden strongly into the fence but within his rhythm and in balance. As soon as they land, horse and rider are immediately moving on towards the next fence.

fences. If you can maintain constant rhythm and prepare yourself for the most economic lines, you won't have to make severe adjustments to your speed, which are also timewasters.

Careful course-walking will help you to save time. Look where you are going and aim to take the shortest route between the fences. Follow the ropes and the direction of the course by looking ahead, not meandering. It is amazing how much time can be wasted by not thinking ahead about the shortest route from fence to fence. Think also about where you will lose time – on a twisty part of the course, on deep going or by taking care around a slippery corner – and decide on suitable galloping stretches, where you can make it up.

When riding the course, avoid unnecessary time penalties by keeping alert on the galloping stretches, rather than dreaming about what a lovely time you are having. If your horse feels tired, abandon all ambitions of achieving the time, as this is when accidents can happen. Instead, concentrate on keeping him between hand and leg and try to give him a breather between fences when you can. When you have completed the course think about your fitness schedule and if necessary seek advice on where you could improve it.

KEEP YOUR COOL

Two of the most unappealing sights in eventing are a horse being rushed towards the finish line in a panic, and a horse being pulled back to a trot as the rider realizes they have gone much too fast. When you do pull up, always do so gradually and on a straight line: abrupt stopping and turning can cause injury.

Problem solving

CHECK YOUR TACK

With a horse that stops at jumps, don't overlook the possibility of tack problems – some horses will stop in certain bits, for example. Stunning was never as brave until I put him in a bit where he was stronger and could take me to a fence. I gradually learned that on the occasions when I felt most comfortable, the bit was actually too strong for him. In order to be forward-thinking, your horse might need to be in a bit that is slightly milder than you would like. There is a happy medium here, though, because if the bit is too mild you will be out of control, which will result in you focusing on your hand – causing restriction – rather than on your leg.

Stopping/napping/running out

Establish why the horse is stopping. It could be pain-related or due to a lack of confidence, or it could be downright naughtiness or that he just doesn't like jumping any more and has had enough. I have ridden a few horses who became prone to stopping: Chaka just needed kicking on, while Western Reef, whom I rode for a few years, benefited greatly from going hunting. However, Cosmopolitan had to be taken back to basics. The first winter I had him he stopped a lot when schooling, even in show jumping; he wasn't hating it, he had just lost confidence – it is the careful horse, like him, who is more prone to losing confidence.

Stunning during an unsuccessful Badminton before we solved his bitting problem. Stunning was strong and needed controlling, but I found that he had more confidence when he felt in charge. We came to a compromise with a pelham.

Cosmopolitan went through a stage where loss of confidence brought about a spree of stopping. Here he is jumping happily through a very testing combination at the Atlanta Olympics.

The horse is resisting control by hollowing, a common fault found on the approach to fences. This horse still manages to jump successfully, despite his resistance – the martingale is clearly having no effect. However, he is likely to improve with training exercises that help him alter his stride pattern more easily.

If you feel your horse is not enjoying what you are asking him to do, try bringing some fun back into his work, through taking a lead or going team-chasing or hunting. Where it is loss of confidence that is causing the problem, then there is nothing for it but to go back to basics, building up his confidence with smaller and less demanding fences. If you think your horse is merely being naughty, don't struggle on your own. The firm hand of a professional trainer can be of great help. Sometimes a temporary change of rider or even just a session with a different rider on board can put a horse back on track.

Rushing and hollowing

Rushing at a fence is a common fault and can be most frustrating. A horse that doesn't look where he is going is neither safe nor pleasant. Try to analyse why he is rushing. Very often it is because he is lacking in confidence or has perhaps been over-faced at some stage and is anxious. Again, I would recommend taking a backward

step and doing plenty of jumping from trot, encouraging the horse to look where he is going and to relax. It could also be that the bitting needs to be looked at, as he may be uncomfortable and trying to get away from the rider's hands.

A horse that persistently rushes is not to be recommended for a young or inexperienced rider as rectifying this problem is quite a challenge. If in doubt, seek professional help.

Backing off

Horses that back off their fences but don't necessarily stop are quite difficult to ride. The most important point is that while you must do everything you can to keep the horse going forwards, you must also maintain a contact. This goes against natural instinct, which is to release the rein on a horse that doesn't want to go forward, but the reality is that by maintaining contact you will give him confidence and security through the reins.

This horse is backing off because he has seen the ditch in front of the fence. His back legs are acting as a brake, but the rider's determination and use of legs, which are in a good position, while maintaining a good balance and contact pays off in getting him over the fence. Having scraped over the fence her troubles are not over, however, as the horse is now neither balanced nor straight enough for the angled roll-top and a rather interesting jump ensues – horse and rider do well to stay together.

At the Competition

How to maximize your chances of success

There is no substitute for the experience to be gained from competitions. I believe strongly in getting young horses to compete early in their careers, but not at a difficult level, so that they experience the competition atmosphere without pressure or being asked any technical questions. The same can apply to riders – it's important to get out and have a crack while not feeling pressurized or being too ambitious.

At first, your intention should be to try to replicate that training feeling by riding in the same way as you would at home. It's also important to have an aim in your mind, even if it's only to complete the competition, or to get one thing right – perhaps in just one phase. Even now, I have a target for every horse in every competition – always in the back of my mind is what I hope to get out of the day – even if it is just for the horse to stay calm in the dressage arena or to take the fences without rushing. You need to have an aim, but you also need to be realistic and be prepared for things to go wrong, even if you really think today is going to be a good day, because this will help you keep your whole approach in perspective. If the horse goes well, you might be disappointed that you didn't win a prize, but make the most of it and be satisfied by what has gone right.

Preparation

I once managed to win a major class without having had time to walk the show-jumping course, but I don't recommend the experience: the feeling of being in a flap and not quite knowing where you're supposed to be going is not a pleasant one and it will transfer itself to your horse.

As soon as you know the times of your classes, work out a structure for the whole day. Competing even just one horse can involve considerable time management. The idea should be to remove all unnecessary pressures so that you can concentrate on the job in hand. To start with, be on time, so that you can work out the competition layout and get ready calmly. This may seem obvious but once you are on the run, it's amazing how difficult it is to settle down and relax.

Sort out your equipment well in advance of the competition, ensuring it is in good condition, clean and packed logically so other people can find things if you need them to. Again the idea is to minimize nasty last-minute surprises; you'd be amazed at how often bridles and jackets get left at home – I even know someone who forgot one of their horses!

Establish a back-up team of helpers who give you confidence rather than make you nervous and who can think for themselves. Don't surround yourself with people who get very nervous themselves or are generally pessimistic.

Your back-up team can make all the difference – surround yourself with people who know what they are doing, are calm and who can think for themselves.

Warm-up

All horses are different in the amount of time they need to settle to a new place; for instance, some produce their best performances after only minimal warm-ups while others need a long time to relax, some like to be hacked while others respond better to lungeing. It is only through experience and experiment that you will discover what best suits your horse.

TRAINING TACTICS

An important part of competing successfully is watching your fellow competitors and asking for their advice. You can learn a lot by seeing how others do it – both good and bad. Remember, though, to be open to the benefits of other people's opinions without feeling obliged to take everything as gospel. Everyone has different requirements and abilities and one of the secrets of success is to know your weaknesses while also being fully aware of your strengths – be prepared to have the confidence not to change something that works for you, no matter what anyone else says. I like to make up my own mind about the cross-country and then seek advice to see if there's anything I have missed. For dressage and show jumping I always find it useful to have some help.

On arrival, take your horse out of the lorry to stretch his legs, have a bit of grass and see where he is. This is particularly important for the more sensitive types. Plan your warm-up, allowing yourself slightly more time than you might anticipate. This will be of benefit if your horse is feeling more excitable than usual and, if everything is going to plan, you can always unwind by giving him a walk on a long rein. This is not the time to decide to change your horse's way of going, or try a different piece of equipment – the idea is to keep everything constant and to simulate being at home. I still occasionally try out new bits at competitions and nearly always regret it.

Do your warm-up in plenty of time so that you can have a break before it's your turn to compete, and don't be tempted to overwork a horse that is going well. This is easy to do under the pressure of competition, but invariably makes them go flat. You will then feel disappointed by the contrast between their performance in the arena and how well they were doing beforehand. How many times have we heard someone say, 'but he was going so well in the warm up...'.

Course walking

TRAINING TACTICS

Don't be one of those people who has to resort to running around the cross-country course – they can't possibly be paying proper attention to it. And resist the temptation to amble around it chatting – it isn't much better. 'Don't do as I do, do as I say…'

A top tip for the show-jumping phase is to allocate time to walk the course. This sounds obvious, but it is surprisingly easy to get involved with other things until it is too late and the course is already in use. It is definitely not sufficient just to watch someone else doing it. However, you should take the opportunity to watch how it is riding and it is well worth asking a more experienced rider if there is anything you should be looking out for.

Cross-country courses

It takes about 45 minutes to walk the average one-day event course, but if you feel you want to walk it twice and also see how a particular fence is riding during the day, you might need to allow an hour and a half or more. Sometimes it is possible to walk the course the night before, which will make for a more relaxing time on the day of the competition.

As you walk the course, bear in mind your own experience and ability, as well as those of your horse. Approach it as if it were a job, thinking about how you're going to tackle it, rather than getting preconceptions about it being easy or hard. Take into account how many straightforward fences there are before the first real test and hope that these will be enough to prepare you and your horse for the first question. When you get to the combinations or more difficult fences, make sure you walk every single route, including long routes, so that you are prepared for any eventuality. Always

have 'plan B' in your mind, because while you should approach a course positively and perhaps aim to take all the most direct routes, it's important to remember that you might have to change your plans. Riding across country involves thinking as you go: you must be aware of how your horse feels and try to read his confidence levels. If he has a bad jump, you might need to regain his confidence and probably your own. In this case, taking a longer, easier route next time is always advisable. While it's an achievement to take all the direct routes, you shouldn't try to be heroic.

Appreciate the siting of each fence and be prepared to balance your horse accordingly. Look out for fences that come after a long gallop, are downhill, on a camber or come quickly after a corner. Watch out for ground conditions – if the going is hard, turns can be slippery, similarly, if there is a deep patch, be ready to go more steadily.

In addition, you need to consider potential distractions, such as the positioning of fence judges or where spectators might be. Fences that take you from light to dark or vice versa, in woods for example, need particular care, and the position of the sun can be of importance – if you are running late in the day, the setting sun shining in your horse's eyes can be a problem.

It's important not to get bogged down with worries about a particular jump; each fence requires your attention and respect. Don't be shy of taking an alternative. What is a 'bogey' fence to one horse and rider won't necessarily be a problem for another; while it's important to ask for an opinion and to find out how a course is riding, it's also important to hold on to your own judgement and not lose your nerve. Three-day events are classic occasions when riders wind each other up about fences because there are so many days in which to worry, whereas at a regular one-day event we get there, walk the course and get on with it.

When walking a cross-country course, always have 'plan B' in mind at a combination. The striding will not always be defined as exactly as you might like, so be prepared either to ride forward to achieve a long distance or to ride more steadily so that your horse can see where to put his feet in a short distance.

Coping with nerves

Show jumping is often the phase that event riders most dread, particularly when it is the finale of a competition, which adds to the tension. Visualize the round in your mind, believe that you will jump clear and try to ride as you normally would at home. This way your nerves will be sensed less by your horse

Everyone suffers from nerves at a competition and we all have that awful feeling when you wish you were somewhere else. This is why some of the most successful riders are not necessarily the most technically gifted but, instead, are those most able to cope with their nerves.

There are lots of reasons for being nervous. Some people are nervous because they want to do well, others because they are frightened of falling off or because they're being watched or maybe even because they're not comfortable with their horse. It's a matter of hoping for the best, but being prepared for the worst and therefore setting yourself up for being able to cope. Again, it all goes back to being organized and surrounding yourself with people who keep calm and give you confidence.

Most riders would say that the churning feeling of butterflies in the stomach prior to starting the cross-country course boosts their performance – there is a theory that the day your nerves leave you is the day to give up. The times I get most nervous are when I feel I should win and when I'm hoping to win, and sometimes when I know I am asking a big question of my horse. I felt quite ill at a three-star three-day event in Germany because I was riding a new horse that I knew wasn't quite ready for the test. The cross country was more difficult than I had expected. My fear was caused by the uncertainty of how the horse was going to cope. In fact, he coped well!

Everyone does something different to deal with their nerves. Some riders need to be on their own to compose themselves; others need the support of their friends and team. Some riders yawn a lot and sleep. American rider Torrance Watkins told me to sing; she sings songs in her head while riding tests but I can't sing! However, I was brought up to control my nerves because if you don't, you can't expect the horse to.

Like many riders, I used to get very tense about the show-jumping phase; I couldn't imagine what it was like to be in the lead at a major event – worse than giving a speech – and it took a long time for me to get over this worry. Something I find helpful is to imagine that I am in a particular situation and I then tell myself that I have to jump a clear round, for example, but at the same time that I must ride in as normal a way as possible. It's no good trying to pretend every competition is a dress rehearsal and never putting yourself under pressure, because one day that pressure will come. You have to allow yourself to be subjected to it by occasionally creating a situation where it matters and learning to cope with it.

I competed a bit as a child in the Pony Club and used to get terribly nervous as a teenager. My mother's approach was expose me to a competitive atmosphere to get me used to the idea that I'd be nervous. Try to recreate a competition experience in your mind in your training, so that you perform a whole dressage test or round of show jumps and pretend it really matters. Visualize the cross-country round and go over it in your imagination so that you are relaxed and confident with what you're going to do.

Self-belief is important and having confidence in one's horse goes a long way. Many a rider has got to the top more through confidence than pure talent. Establish confidence by setting realistic targets, by feeling well-prepared – which means knowing the dressage test and having jumped over similar heights and types of fences – presenting yourself well and by having pride in your horse. It's easy for your confidence to spiral down if you're following a top rider, but don't worry about what everyone else is doing – in eventing you are there to compete to the best of your ability. Often your best on a certain day isn't good enough to win, but it doesn't matter.

TRAINING TACTICS

Acknowledge your nerves and then work out how best to minimize them and how to make them work for you. Exposure to competition experience is the best way to learn how to control your nerves and to develop a system that works for you. Ginny Elliot told me to imagine when competing that I was in the field at home, doing a round of show jumps with no one else there. This has proven to be excellent advice.

TIPS FOR PREPARATION

■ For the novice horse or rider a good competition experience is more important than being placed

■ Set yourself an achievable aim for each competition and be pleased with any successes

■ Have a complete and detailed timetable for every part of a competition day

■ Make a list of everything you need to take with you and check and pack all equipment carefully the day before

■ Take a supportive and efficient back-up team and make sure they know what they're expected to do

■ Never skimp on preparation, including thorough walking of the show-jumping and cross-country courses

■ Warm-up in plenty of time and don't overdo it

■ Always allow yourself more time for each task than you think you will need

CROSS-COUNTRY TIPS

■ Look at each fence, even the 'easy' ones, and assess each route carefully

■ Always have an alternative route planned out

■ Don't be heroic and then regret an almost clear round

■ Ask the opinion of more experienced riders, but remember to take into account your level of experience and ability

■ If your horse has a bad experience, work on regaining his confidence through schooling before your next outing

Problem solving

If you are having performance problems with your horse, remember that most faults and forms of resistance are caused by the rider. Think about whether your horse is uncomfortable with his bit or saddle, or whether his back is sore. Think also about what you are doing – are you sitting crooked, or against the movement, or are you being heavy-handed? Are you riding forward and positively, or are you just sitting lightly and nervously and not helping?

The hollow horse

With a horse that sticks his head in the air and hollows his back, sit as lightly as possible while maintaining a degree of leg pressure, and concentrate on riding him in a rounder outline than you would normally be aiming for. So when you go in the arena – the moment at which a horse will tend to put his head up – the fact that you have worked on him being more rounded in your preparation should result in him being in approximately the right outline. It is important when working deep to achieve this softness, that he is deep from the base of his neck and not simply flexing from the

Work a hollow horse more deeply and rounder than you would normally before you go in to the arena, and you will find that the hollowness can be disguised with this outline compromise.

poll area and that he is working through from behind. In the arena, it's equally important to keep your seat light and soft and I would advise maximizing your use of the corners and turns to re-create a soft outline whenever possible.

The overbent horse

Overbending is another common fault, which can be taken seriously by some judges. A priority is to ensure you ride your horse in a mild and comfortable bit that encourages him to take the contact. It is also worth remembering that a horse that is working poll-high – with his poll being the highest point of his neck – physically cannot be overbent. Before a dressage test, I do a lot of my warm-up in a long outline, encouraging my horse to take a contact, then I gradually work him into a more collected uphill frame. When in the arena I concentrate on riding the horse from behind into the poll-high outline, still maintaining contact. Remember to allow your horse to take your hand forwards at every possible opportunity.

With both overbending and hollowness, it is important that the rider uses the leg to minimize these faults, as often they originate from horses who are not working from behind.

A horse that is being worked in a long and low outline cannot get overbent. With the horse that has a tendency towards this fault, warm him up in as long an outline as possible, encouraging him to take your hand forwards.

The lacklustre horse

The horse that goes 'dead' in the arena can be very disappointing. In this case, the rider needs to establish a bolder approach and perhaps cut warm-up time to a bare minimum in order to preserve some freshness. I used to ride a horse called Western Reef, who was a classic example of a horse that would loose interest if the rider wasn't careful. Eventually, I devised a system of warming him up 90 minutes before the test, in order to get him relaxed, and then getting on him again only 10 minutes before the test and riding him briskly straight down to the arena. I would then ride him into the arena in a lighter, less disciplined manner, aiming more for freedom and forwardness than for obedience and precision.

The lonely horse

Some horses don't like being on their own, especially if the arena is a long way from the warm-up area. You can work on this at home, but one solution, which my mother used to use, is to get someone to come and watch the test, holding another horse. Although not as easy to achieve nowadays, this can work particularly well if you have the misfortune of being last to go and everyone else has disappeared!

The nervous horse

You can't force a horse to produce a good test and there is always a danger in working a horse hard of winding them up more or making their muscles uncomfortable.

Stunning, pictured winning at Chatsworth, had a particular tendency towards nerves. Working him hard was not the solution – we just had to find ways of keeping him occupied and, therefore, relaxed at a competition. With any nervous horse, it is largely a case of trial and error with a variety of activities to find one that will help him cope with the atmosphere.

Stunning is a particularly nervous horse; he tends to blow his nose and hold his breath. No amount of work will get him to relax. I have found that the best approach is a psychological one. For example, if your horse is always nervous about going into a dressage arena, it may be that he finds the isolation unnerving. You just have to experiment with ways of overcoming this. Spend lots of time relaxing him at the competition – this doesn't mean overworking him – and perhaps mix lungeing, hacking and schooling work with a bit of time out of the lorry, to allow him to absorb the atmosphere.

The electric horse

The 'electric' horse can, oddly enough, gain security by being ridden positively. Ballincoola, who was second at Bramham in 2003, is a hot horse. When I first rode him, he wouldn't accept the leg at all and would be over-sensitive and over-reactive. With time, he began to accept my leg and gain a security from it which, somewhat ironically, has had the effect of making him lazy. Now I have to kick him, whereas once this would have been like an electric shock to him. The rider's instinct on an explosive horse is to take the leg away, whereas the reverse is what is nearly always required to produce a better and more relaxed performance.

Highland Lad, pictured here at Burghley, was a lively ride but he gained security – and even changed personality – when he was ridden positively. Instinct tells you to take your leg away from a flighty horse, but in fact the security of being between hand and leg will often be what is needed to relax him.

Get Your Horse Fit

Fitness is important for the welfare of both horse and rider. It is only fair on the horse to get him to a reasonable level of fitness for competition. Not only will he find being tired an unpleasant experience, which may make him less enthusiastic next time out, but being unfit can so easily result in injury, leading to a boring and frustrating recovery period. There is also the safety aspect to consider – a horse that is full of energy is less likely to make a misjudgement than a tired one, particularly towards the end of a cross-country course.

As courses have become more demanding at all levels, we've also all been made increasingly aware of the importance of rider fitness. It must be a really horrible feeling to be desperate for your round to be over because you are gasping for breath, and it is dangerous, too. Professional riders have an advantage here because we're riding so many horses every day so keep naturally fit for the job, but in recent years we have been made to acknowledge how important it is to be as fit as we can over and above this. For the one-horse, working rider, who simply has not the time to spend in the saddle, some additional fitness work – perhaps going swimming, running or spending time the gym – can be of major benefit and makes for a much more enjoyable experience when riding across country.

From field to first competition

The most important thing to remember about achieving proper fitness in the horse is that it's a slow process. This can make it difficult for part-time or working riders who may not be able to pursue the process as thoroughly as they would like, but there are no short cuts to fitness and if any stages are missed in the slow preparatory work, you may find that things go wrong further down the road, when it is too late.

From getting the horse out of the field, where he has been having a holiday, to going to his first competition of the season, I reckon to allow 8–10 weeks. The extra two weeks are a safety net in case something goes wrong – a minor injury or bad weather. Two weeks on box rest due to injury or days only going on the horsewalker because of heavy snow does not count as part of the fitness process!

I plan to spend 2–4 weeks walking, starting with about 30 minutes and building up to about 90 minutes. Four weeks is the maximum and this does depend on how unfit the horse had become during his break, and also on his temperament as some horses become frustrated when they only do walking exercise.

For both his physical and mental wellbeing, your horse needs to get as much opportunity as possible for moving around when he is not being exercised. It's best that a horse lives out as much as possible, particularly during the walking period – a simple daily hack is not enough to alleviate boredom and it is not good for him to be in the stable for 23 hours a day. My horses are turned out every day during the season,

Being turned out in the field every day will greatly enhance a horse's mental and physical well being. Plenty of turn-out time not only aids fitness and relaxation, it usually makes for a much happier horse.

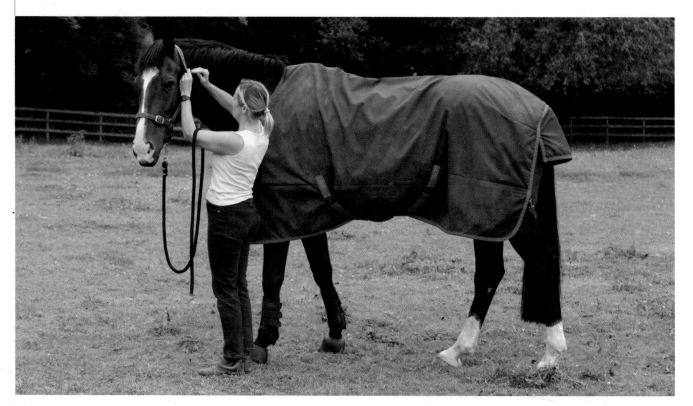

If you are lucky enough to have access to a horsewalker, this makes a great fitness supplement, which adds to the variety of the horse's day and aids circulation. It also means that you can get on with another job while the horse is still getting some exercise warming up or cooling down.

several of them living out at night as well. It helps their fitness and circulation and it's great for their minds. Many yards now have a horsewalker, and you could supplement his daily hack with a 30-minute session on that.

After 2–4 weeks you can introduce trot work, either in a schooling arena or out on a hack in the countryside. This should be increased gradually over two weeks, during which time you should be able to detect that the horse's muscles are strengthening and hardening. Also during this period, and where facilities permit, hillwork can be used increasingly and it is of great benefit. I don't generally trot my horses on roads, but I see no harm in trotting up the odd hill if necessary.

Gentle cantering follows at the end of the two trotting weeks and, again, this should be increased over the next two weeks so that jumping and faster work can be gradually mixed in at the end of the fortnight. The first two weeks of canter work at a steady, schooling pace will gradually increase the horse's strength and lung capacity, with the emphasis on it being a slow building-up process. If you hurry the cantering in the early stages, it will inevitably result in muscle stiffness, which in turn means your horse will have to have days off to recover, and this will negate the work already done and protract the fitness programme. Before you introduce faster work, your horse should be finding it easy to canter at a steady pace for two four-minute sessions.

After eight weeks, faster canter work can be introduced in conjunction with jumping exercises, and again there should be two weeks of this, incorporating a cross-country schooling session, before your first event. Your fast-work programme will depend on facilities available and the level of competition at which you are aiming, but for the novice horse the odd faster canter will suffice. I rarely take my novice horses to the gallops. At this level in eventing, some horses don't need to be over-fittened as they become too fit and fresh for what is required of them.

For fast work you need to find good ground, because cantering on poor surfaces can have a cumulatively serious effect on a horse's legs and shorten his competitive career. Hard ground can cause sprains and strains to the tendons, especially if it is also rough – imagine turning your own ankle when walking on ridged ground – and

If the surface is suitable, I allow my horses to roll in the school after a session – provided there are no other horses there. It will make them feel comfortable and relaxed after working.

A WEEK IN THE LIFE OF ONE OF MY NOVICE HORSES

Monday: day off

Tuesday: hacking, fun ride, hillwork (1–1½ hours)

Wednesday: horsewalker (30 minutes) and school work (45 minutes)

Thursday: hack or horsewalker session (30 minutes) followed by some canter work

Friday: horsewalker (30 minutes) or hack (1 hour) and schooling/jumping (45–50 minutes)

Saturday: a hack and a lungeing session (the latter could be substituted by a schooling session if dressage revision is necessary)

Sunday: competition

asking a horse to work in deep, sticky mud can cause muscle strains.

It's important to vary the work during any given fitten- ing week, not only for your horse's fitness but for his mental health, too. It's good for morale to have constant variety and it's particularly important to keep the event horse interested in his work, bearing in mind the load he has to cope with. Therefore plan your week not only with building all-round fitness in mind, but also keeping him entertained.

Hillwork versus interval training

Once you have started doing fast work, you can increase your horse's overall fitness using either hill- work or interval training. Which you choose will largely depend on your facilities and the kind of horse, but both have been proven to work well.

In interval training, periods of canter work are inter- spersed with periods of rest, and the length of cantering time can be increased gradually, depending on what level of competition you're aiming for. For instance, two five-minute canters at a strong pace, interspersed with a three-minute walk, per session, is plenty for a horse about to go around a novice course. Alternatively, if you're lucky enough to live in a hilly area, a couple of canters up a hill per session would again be more than enough for the average novice horse. Hillwork is a great natural way of getting your horse fit.

The bonus of an all-weather gallop is that it provides consistent going, which will help preserve your horse's legs when he is undergoing serious fitness training.

Taking fitness a step futher

For the next stages in your horse's career, I advise sourcing a good all-weather gallop, preferably uphill, especially when preparing for a three-day event, as this not only provides consistent ground on which to gallop in all weather conditions, but is a forgiving surface for your horse's legs when he is undergoing an increasing work load.

However fit you want your horse to be, the emphasis should always be on adjusting the programme to suit the horse, not the other way around. It undoubtedly takes more time and work to get a less athletic, less quality horse fit. In this case, effort must be made to find some hills, but if these are not readily available, devise a strict interval training programme and make sure that when the horse is being ridden he is really working properly under you. Often a horse of lesser quality will have a more laid back temperament and won't work himself naturally. Commonsense should tell you whether your horse is comfortable with the work he has been asked to do.

HEALTH CHECKS

Physiotherapy is now widely recognized as a crucial part of a horse's training programme. My horses have their backs checked at the beginning of the year and are also assessed at the end of the season before being turned out. I am a believer in regular physiotherapy throughout the season because the physio can spot something the rider won't, or has come to accept, but which may be affecting the horse's performance. Small adjustments and the use of gentle massaging machines, such as Equissage, can result in the most dramatic changes in the horse's performance. Stunning, having had a tough career in the racing world, followed by eight years of eventing, is particularly receptive to physiotherapy and his performance has been greatly enhanced by his being comfortable.

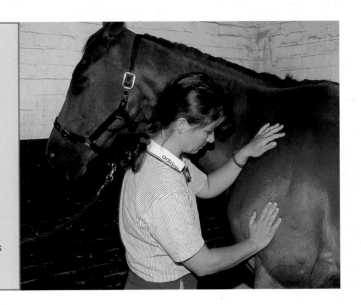

Horses for courses

Different horses benefit from different types of work and you need to think about what sort of horse you have when planning his programme. For instance, Stunning, a light-framed New Zealand Throughbred ex-racehorse, only needs two-thirds of the work that Moon Man, a heavier Irish-bred horse, needs to get the same end result.

The more Thoroughbred types – like Stunning, who I've always said only has to look at a hill to be fit – have an active brain and in-built energy and are much easier to get into condition. This is a considerable advantage, because the less work a horse has to do to get fit, the less wear and tear there is on his body. Even while he is on holiday, the Thoroughbred type with an active mental outlook will tend to lose less fitness than the sleepier, heavier type.

The Thoroughbreds in my yard are fittened by galloping them up hills at increasing

Stunning is a light-framed little Thoroughbred, an ex-racehorse with huge stamina. He was easy to get fit and always a willing.ride

speeds an increasing number of times. However, when preparing a more middleweight, laid-back model of horse, such as Moon Man or Chaka, much more careful consideration is required. With them, I combine short, sharp hillwork sessions with long, slow canter work, to work on their wind fitness and stamina. This not only achieves physical freshness but also mental alertness.

It is important for horses with less quality to become accustomed to galloping for a given length of time. Like human athletes during physical exertion, horses can reach a barrier at which they'd like to pull up; they will drop the bridle and you have to persuade them to go on. Some horses need to have psychological training to learn that it's possible to overcome that barrier, but others won't even notice it. Stunning would never stop until asked, but Chaka, for instance, when doing interval training of three 10-minute canters, developed the habit of pulling himself up after 10 minutes across country, so I established a programme that combined two 12-minute canters with hillwork. As a result, he became mentally more able to accept the full length of a four-star three-day event, such as Badminton.

Moon Man's relaxed personality meant it was difficult at first to tell whether he was fit enough. He is a big, generous horse and it took time for him to develop a core fitness and strength.

With Moon Man it was a matter of experimenting to achieve the required level of fitness. He would appear to have done all the necessary work in the build-up to a three-day event and would feel 100 per cent fit, and yet he wasn't able to cope once he got to a four-star event. With hindsight, two factors have come to light. Firstly, as he is a very straightforward and trainable horse, he got to four-star level before he was physically ready, which meant he lacked a core fitness and strength. Secondly, his relaxed personality and co-operative nature meant that the fact he was doing less work went unnoticed. As he is never rebellious or difficult and just does what he is told, I would tend to ride him and put him away without thinking whether he had actually worked hard.

When I took him to Badminton, he wasn't feeling 100 per cent and pulled himself up on the cross-country. Then at Burghley, when he started to feel the same sensation, he thought, 'This is where we pull up', and ground to a halt. I decided to review his fitness programme and introduced some long, slow canter work at home, either in the school or in the field when the going was suitable, and this was done in between his fast hill work sessions. I concentrated on his stamina and every time he worked at home, great care was taken to establish that he was putting in the effort; when he was galloping or doing fast work, I would take him just that little bit quicker, galloping him up hill faster and in company.

This increased work load was obviously a risk on his long-term soundness, but I felt very strongly that he had to be fitter in order to perform at top level. In Moon Man's favour he has good conformation and, being light on his feet, he has come through the work and profited from it. He is now over the mental barrier and at the four-star event in Kentucky in 2003, where he finished third, he won the award for the best-conditioned horse throughout the competition.

FITNESS TIPS

- An unfit horse is an unsafe horse

- You owe it to your horse to be fit too

- Fitness work can never be rushed or skimped

- Allow more time than you think you need to get your horse fully fit

- Keep your horse out in the field as much as possible and limit the time he is confined to a stable

- Variety will keep your horse's interest in his work

- Gradually build up to fast work to ensure your horse has the stamina, strength and mental outlook to cope

- Avoid injuries by taking one step at a time and never overdoing your horse's training

- Consider having regular visits from a physiotherapist to identify possible physical problems early on

- Suit your programme to your horse, not the other way around

- Continually assess your horse to ensure your fitness programme is working

Index

Page numbers in *italic* refer to picture captions

accuracy fences 96–111, *96–111*
Achselschwang 26
aids 39, *44*
Andrew, Frank 24
angles 60, *60*, 96
Anstee, Georgina *14*
Apter, George 24; Jayne *19*, 24
Archangel *35*
arrowheads 54, 96, *100*
Atlanta Olympics *20*, 24, 26

backing off 137, *137*
back-up team 140, *140*, 145
Badminton 17, 20, 24, 26, 27
balance 38–9, 46, 68; banks and steps *78–9*, *82–3*; downhill fences 80; drops 84, 86; jumping 102
Ballincoola 10, 27, 149
banks 74, *74–83*, 110; out of water *116*
Barcelona Olympics 17
Barclay Square 27
Bateson, Sally *14*
bend *40*, *43*
Blarney Castle 26
Blenheim 26
Boekelo 26, 27
bounces 96, *103, 105–7*; into water *120–1*
Bradwell, Judy 15
Brakewell, Jeanette *7*
Bramham 10, 26, 27
Breisner, Yogi *7*
Briarlands Pippin 16, 17
British Intermediate 26, 27
British Open *19*, 26, 27
bullfinch *103*
Burghley 16, 20, 26, 27, *149*
Burgie 26, 27
Burton, Nick 17

canter 36, *36–7*, 153, *154*; polework 46; rider's position *68*; water jumps *113, 118*
Chaka 17, *18*, 19–20, 24, 26, 134, 156, 157, *157*
Chambers, Steven *14*
Chantilly 26
Chatsworth 27, *148*
circles *40*
Clark, Lorna 70
Coastal Ties 27
coffins 122–3, *122–7*
Compiègne 26
confidence, loss of 134, 136

contact, rider/horse 31, 33, *33*, 72, *72*
Cook, Kristina 17
co-ordination 46
corners 54, 60, *61*, 96, *108–9*
Cosmopolitan 24, 26, 134, *135*
Cotter, Sheila 34
counter canter 36, 39, *44*
cross country 13, 54, 66–137, 145; training tactics 51, 102, 105
crosspoles 51, 52, *53*, *57*

Diable Au Corps 27
ditches 58, *58–9*
Dixon, Karen *20*, 70
dressage 10, 13–14, 16, 29, 39; competition 48–9; test 31, 48–9
drops 84–7, *84–7*

Elliot, Ginny 17, 145
European Championships 7, *15*, 16, 17, 26, 27
Eventer's Grand Prix 26, *80*
eventing 9–11, 14, 16, 25

Faerie Diadem 26
Faerie Sovereign 16, 17, 26
fences 58, *58–9*, 88–101, *88–101*; accuracy 96–111, *96–111*; approach and position 88, *89–91*, 96; backing off 137, *137*; bounces 96, *103, 105–7*; combination *80–1*; double *103, 108–9*; downhill *80*; guidance poles *98*; light, changes of 128, *130–1*; roofed 128, *129*; rushing 136–7; spooky 62, 128, *128–31*; stride-bounce combination *103*; turns 54, 96; water 112–21, *112–21 see also* jumping
fitness 151–9
flatwork 29–49
flexibility 46
flying change *45*
Fox-Pitt, Alicia *12*; Andrew *12, 13*; Laurella *12*; Marietta 11–12, *13, 14*, 15–16, *148*; Oliver *12*
Funnell, Pippa *7*, 17

gallop 34, 155, *155*, 156, 157
Gatcombe *19*, 20, 25
Green, Lucinda *108*
gridwork 54, *55, 56–7*, 57
guidance poles *98*
Guinness, Hon Mary 24, *24*

hacking 31
half-pass *43*
Hawtree, Melanie *14*
Hazlem, Simon *14*
health checks 155
Highland Lad 26, 27, *149*
Highland Spirit 27
hillwork 154, *154*, 155, 156
Hoeg, Clea *14*
hollowing 136–7, *136*, 146–7, *146*
horsewalkers 153, *153*
hunting 12, 13, 15
hunting seat *84*

Igor de Cluis 27
Ildalgo 27
interval training 155, 157

jumping 12–13, 31, 39, 50–65, 68–71; banks and steps *76–83*; drops 84–7, *84–7*; flying change *45*; from light to dark, 130; rhythm 52, 54, 57, 68; riding to speed 54, *132*; straightness 51, 52, *53*, 54, *56–7, 78 see also* fences

Kentucky *13*, 27
Knowlton Corona *12*

Lane Fox, George *10*
Law, Graham *14*; Leslie *7*, 24
leg-yielding *42*
light, changes of 128, *130–1*
Lismore Lord Charles 26
Lithgow, Colonel *14*
Lloyd-Thomas, Roland *14*
Loch Alan 26
long rein *34*
loneliness 148
Luhmuhlen 27
Lummen 27
lungeing 51

Macaire, Susanna 16, 17
manoeuvrability 39
martingale *14*
massage 155
Moody, Hannah *16*

Moon Man *13, 21*, 24–5, 26, 27, 31, *31*, 156, *158*, 159
Moonstone *123*
Morris, Andrea *14*
Mostly Mischief 26
Mr Beluga 26
Mulligan's Shenanigans 26
muscle tone 46

napping 134
National Championships 26
Necarne Castle 26
nerves, coping with 144–5
nervous horses 148–9

outline 38–45, *38–45*
overbending 147, *147*
over-training 30
owl holes 128

paces 34–6, *34–7*; transitions 38, *38–41*
Parsonage, Gary 70
Payne, Lucy *10*
Phillipps, Vere 24
physiotherapy 155
Pie In The Sky II 26
pimples 96
polework 39, 46, *46*, 51, 52, 55
Potts, Jackie 17
preparation 140–1, 145
Princess Royal *19*
The Professor 27
Punchestown 26

Railton, Jamie *14*
Ramus, Alexandra *14*
reinback 39, *44*
rewards 30, *30*, 46
rhythm 46, 52, 54, 57, 68
rider's fitness 151
rider's position 31, 32–3, *32–3, 41*, 48, 146; cross-country 70–1, *70–1*; drops 84, *84*; jumping fences 88, *89–91*, 96
rolling *153*
running out 134
rushing 136–7

Sandillon 27
Saumur 27
Scarvagh 27
Scottish Open 26, 27
self-belief 144, 145
self-carriage 46
Shear H$_2$0 24
shoulder-in *42*
showjumping 10, 62–3, 64–5, 142–5

Skinner, Judy *10*
slipping the reins 72
speed, riding to 54, 132–3
sponsorship 16, 17
spooky fences, 128
Springleaze Macaroo 27
Stark, Ian *20*
Steadfast 15–16, *15*, 19, 24, 26
steps 74, *74–83*
stirrup length 68, *70–1*
stopping 134
straightness *41*, 68, 69, *78, 82*
stride bounce combination 56, *103, 107*
Stunning 17, 19, *19*, 24, 26, 27, *103*, 134, *134, 148*, 149, 155, 156, *156*, 157
sunken roads 122–3, *122–7*

tack and equipment *14*, 134, 140, 145, 146
Tamarillo *11, 22*, 24, *24, 25*, 26, 27, *86*
Thirlestane *18*, 20
Thomastown 26
Todd, Mark 24
Tom Cruise 27
transitions 38, *38–41, 49*
trot 35, *35*, 46, 153
Turner, Sir Michael 17
turn-out 152–3, *152*
turns *40*, 54, 96

Uncle Sam II 26

visualization 48, 144, 145

walk 34, *34*
walking the course 62, 142–3, *143*, 145
Wallow *10*, 27
warming up 62, 63, *63*, 140–1, *141*, 145
warm-up 48, 68, 145
water: banks out of *116*; bounce into *120–1*; drops into *87*, 112–13, *112–14*, 114, *118*, *120–1*; jumping 112–13, *112–21*
Watkins, Torrance 144
Watson, Gill 16
Watson, Greg 17
weather 143
Western Reef 26, 27, 134, 148
Windsor 26, 27
World Championship 20
World Cup *19*
World Games *11, 22*, 24, 27